The
Lathe Book

The Lathe Book

A complete guide for the wood craftsman

ERNIE CONOVER

The Taunton Press

Cover photo: SLOAN HOWARD

Taunton
BOOKS & VIDEOS
for fellow enthusiasts

First printing: September 1993
Printed in the United States of America

A FINE WOODWORKING Book

FINE WOODWORKING® is a trademark of The Taunton Press, Inc.,
registered in the U.S. Patent and Trademark Office.

The Taunton Press, 63 South Main Street, Box 5506, Newtown,
CT 06470-5506

Library of Congress Cataloging-in-Publication Data

Conover, Ernie.
    The lathe book / Ernie Conover.
        p.   cm.
    "A Fine Woodworking book."
    Includes index.
    ISBN 1-56158-057-0
    1. Lathes.   2. Turning.   I. Title.
TT201.C66   1993   93-28008
684'.083—dc20   CIP

I dedicate this book to my mother and father. Both talented artists, they have always nurtured a quest for knowledge and love of art, craft and history.

Contents

ACKNOWLEDGMENTS

Writing a book is a big undertaking, and I would like to thank the following people who were extremely generous of their time and long-suffering in reviewing material and discussing their opinions: Michael Dunbar, David Ellsworth, Dave Hout, Darrel Nish of Craft Supplies USA, Larry Olson of Delta International Machinery Corp., Rude Osolnik and Norm Vandal. The following people shared specialized knowledge and product information: Mark Blocher of Divine Brothers Company, Mike Carrol of Formax Manufacturing Corp., Tim Clay of Oneway Manufacturing, John Cochrane of J4 Consulting Services, Alan Dinning of SKF Bearings, Gerry Glaser of Glaser Engineering Company, cabinetmaker John Leeke, Richard Lukes of Beech Street Tool Works, Mike Nelson of Airstream Dust Helmets, Brad Packard of Packard Woodworks, Tony Walker of Robert Sorby Ltd., and Dan Walter of Eagle America. I'd particularly like to thank Delta International for supplying the Delta 46-700 on which many of the photos in this book were shot.

I'd also like to thank all the folks at The Taunton Press, with special mention to Helen Albert, John Lively and my editor, Peter Chapman. At the outset of this project, Peter traveled here to Ohio to take my week-long Woodturning Tools and Techniques course. His input to this book has been invaluable since he has unique dual qualifications—the talents of a skilled editor and the abilities of a respectable turner.

My father, E. R. Conover, Jr., deserves a "run hard and put away wet" award. Almost daily he reviewed my work with a patient, practiced eye, gained through 50 years of engineering experience and a great love of anything to do with lathes. And, finally, thanks to my wife and family for allowing me the time to write this book, and for reviewing manuscripts and filtering out my corny puns.

INTRODUCTION

In this book I will share with you my love of the woodturning lathe. This is a book with a difference, because it doesn't focus on the lathe to the exclusion of all other woodworking. Rather, it treats the lathe as another essential tool in the woodworking shop—a tool that can expand your woodworking horizon and add pizzazz to your work. The lathe is a tool that all woodworkers need to be more familiar with, since at some point your woodworking projects will require turned parts.

Turning books generally speak to dedicated turners who pursue turning to the exclusion of all other forms of woodworking. But most woodworkers are interested in turning only enough to use the lathe in their general woodworking. Additionally, most turning books miss the mark because they never really teach you to turn. They talk about equipment, philosophy and history, but never truly teach turning.

With this in mind, I've tried to write a woodturning book that speaks to all woodworkers and gives the information necessary to be able to employ turning in furniture making. A second objective is to offer advice on buying, maintaining, modifying and repairing lathes—a good part of the book is devoted to the intricacies of lathes and their accessories.

I grew up at the lathe, and I've been turning both wood and metal since I was 12 years old. I understand lathes and how they work. For many years, my father and I owned a company that produced a lathe we co-designed—the Conover Lathe. An outgrowth of our lathe-manufacturing business is Conover Workshops, a woodworking school that my wife and I now run year round. In 16 years of running the school, I've taught hundreds of people to turn and have a fair sense of where the hurdles are in the learning process.

It's my firm belief that most people have the ability to turn, but this skill has been buried deep inside during the process of growing up. In many cases, it has been masked by fear and dull tools. If you read through the next 200 pages or so, I think you'll be able to regain your instinctive turning skill and have some fun in the process. I look forward to this book starting a revolution in your workshop.

CHAPTER 1
The Lathe

The woodturning lathe is a simple workshop tool that can greatly expand your woodworking horizon. If you want to shape table legs, chair spindles and bed posts or add embellishment to your furniture in the form of drawer pulls, cabinet knobs and finials, then you need a lathe. And if you want to make bowls, plates, stool seats, tabletops and lidded boxes, a lathe is an indispensable machine.

Lathes come in all makes and sizes, from benchtop models to industrial heavyweights, but the basic design is the same on all lathes. A rigid bed supports a stationary headstock and a tailstock that can be moved to accommodate wood blanks of various lengths. A motor turns a spindle mounted in the headstock, which in turn drives the work. The drawing on the facing page shows a composite woodturning lathe combining the features of many lathes. I call this lathe "Everylathe" because there is no lathe that would have all of the features shown.

The first part of this chapter is a primer on lathe construction and lathe anatomy to help you choose a lathe. The type of lathe you need will depend to a large extent on the kind of work you plan to do. For example, if you want to turn only a few chair legs occasionally, a light-duty lathe will be more than adequate, whereas heavy bowl turning will require a much sturdier and larger machine. However, there are

Everylathe

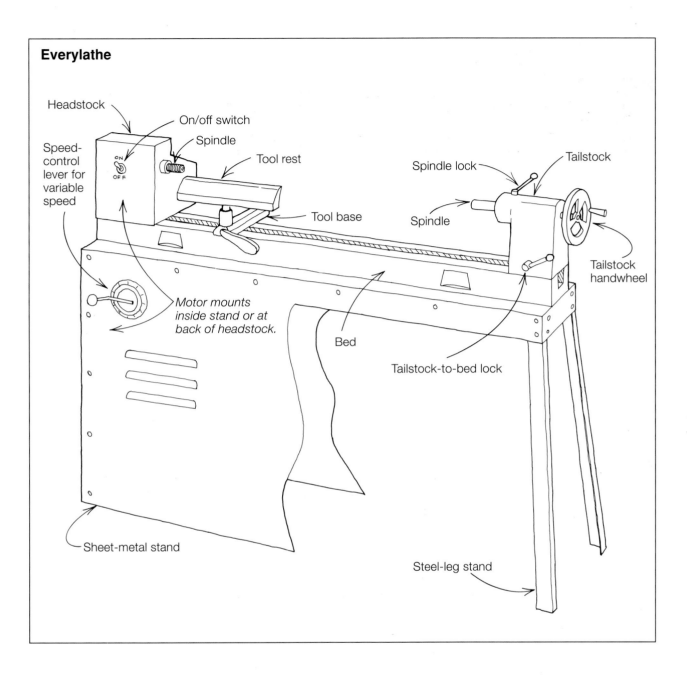

Headstock

On/off switch

Spindle

Tool rest

Speed-control lever for variable speed

ON
OFF

Tool base

Spindle lock

Tailstock

Spindle

Motor mounts inside stand or at back of headstock.

Tailstock handwheel

Bed

Tailstock-to-bed lock

Sheet-metal stand

Steel-leg stand

certain desirable features you should look for in any lathe, and I've drawn attention to these throughout this section to help you make an intelligent buying decision. The second part of the chapter explains what you need to consider when setting up a lathe, and the chapter concludes with some important advice on lathe safety.

Lathe construction

The earliest lathes were made of wood (see the sidebar on pp. 8-9 for a discussion on the history of the lathe), and the use of wood as a bed material has survived right up to the present day. Much more common today, however, are lathes with all-metal parts. The four basic lathe-construction materials you're likely to encounter are cast iron, fabricated steel, cast aluminum and zinc, and extruded aluminum.

Cast iron

Cast iron is a time-honored material for lathe construction that's still hard to beat. The inherent mass of the material provides maximum stability and ensures minimal vibration. Most woodworking machinery is cast from grade-25 grey iron, which has a nice balance between strength, damping effect and machinability.

Top-quality lathes are made with a heavy cast-iron headstock, tailstock and tool-rest assembly. A lathe with these cast-iron parts mounted on a wooden bed is known as a "High Wycombe lathe," after the lathes that were popular with turners who turned furniture parts around High Wycombe, England, until the early part of this century. Many of the photographs in this book are of a High Wycombe lathe that I co-designed.

Economy lathes are also sometimes made with cast-iron parts, but the castings are usually light and the surfaces are often not machined smooth. Any roughness in the sliding surfaces can make adjustments awkward because the tool rest and tailstock tend to jam.

Fabricated steel

Fabricated lathes are made by welding together pieces of structural steel. Fabrication first became popular in the late 1950s as a cheaper alternative to iron castings. Its biggest advantage is that little or no tooling costs are required, which makes fabrication particularly well suited to small production runs where amortizing the costs of patterns for castings would be difficult. Another advantage is that fabricated headstocks are easier to machine than cast-iron headstocks. On the down side, steel has poor damping qualities compared to grade-25 cast iron, though I have turned on some fabricated lathes that performed reasonably well.

A lathe with cast-iron parts provides maximum stability for all turning operations.

Cast aluminum and zinc

Parts such as pulleys, knobs and handwheels are often made from cast aluminum or zinc. These are often called die castings, because the low melting temperature of aluminum and zinc allows them to be cast in metal molds or dies. Die castings are almost perfect directly from the mold and require little machining. The low weight of aluminum makes it a good material for pulleys because balancing is less of a problem than with cast-iron pulleys.

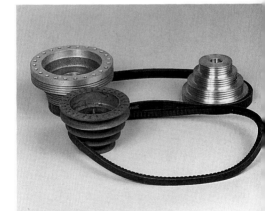

Cast aluminum is often used for the pulley on the headstock spindle.

Extruded aluminum

You occasionally see a lathe made of extruded aluminum. Although extrusions can be tempered, the alloys used for the process are soft and gummy compared to cast aluminum, cast iron or structural steel. This softness, and the tendency of raw aluminum to turn anything it touches black, is somewhat ameliorated by anodizing, a plating process that puts a thin, hard coat of aluminum oxide on the surface of the metal. However, dents that go through the anodized surface into the soft aluminum substrate are a potential problem.

We're seeing more and more extrusions in woodworking machinery today—you may well have some in your shop yourself. Although extrusions are acceptable for miniature lathes and parts of lathes, I'm not convinced that they are suitable for an entire full-sized machine. The decision to buy a lathe made principally of extrusions would depend on how much and what type of use you intend to subject it to.

Hybrid designs

Most lathes available today are hybrid designs, incorporating two or more of the construction materials outlined above. A common design is a cast-iron headstock, tailstock and tool base mounted on a structural-steel bed or, on economy lathes, on hollow-steel tubing. Steel stampings, sheet metal, aluminum extrusions and plastic are often used for stands, belt covers and knobs.

The Delta 46-700 features a cast-iron headstock, tailstock, tool base and bed on a stamped-steel stand.

The Record Coronet No. 1 is a good-quality benchtop lathe. (Photo courtesy of Record Tools Inc.)

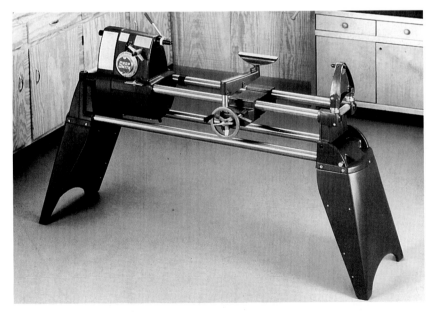

The Shopsmith Mark V is a multipurpose tool that makes a very good lathe. (Photo courtesy of Shopsmith, Inc.)

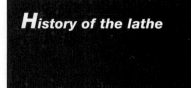

The lathe is one of the oldest woodworking tools, although the actual details of its use in pre-history is largely a matter of conjecture. The earliest lathes were nothing more than two wood frames mounted on a bed formed by two wood planks. Each of the frames, or "poppits," carried a metal point, which allowed turning between centers. Both of the points were "dead" centers, since neither was under power, and did double duty holding the work and acting as the bearings on which the work rotated. To minimize friction, the centers were lubricated with grease before the work was mounted.

Power was provided by the operator. The most common setup (at least in Europe) was the pole lathe. A sapling was secured above the lathe (or the lathe was simply placed under a tree with the right branch) and a rope was tied to the end of it. The rope was then wrapped once around the work and passed between the rails of the bed, ending in a loop. The operator put one foot in the loop. By stepping down the work was powered and a cut was made. Stepping up released tension on the rope, and the sapling provided spring tension to return everything to the starting point.

The work spun backwards during this return stroke, necessitating moving the turning tool back out of contact with the work. In medieval Europe, a long bow was used instead of a sapling to provide the spring tension to return the rope.

A variant of the pole lathe was the bow lathe, which is prevalent to this day in India, Afghanistan and the Far East. The bow lathe was used for small-scale work and substituted a bow for the pole. The bow string was wrapped once directly around the work, which compressed the bow a bit. The work was powered by sawing the bow back and forth. Bowing was generally done with the right hand while the tool was

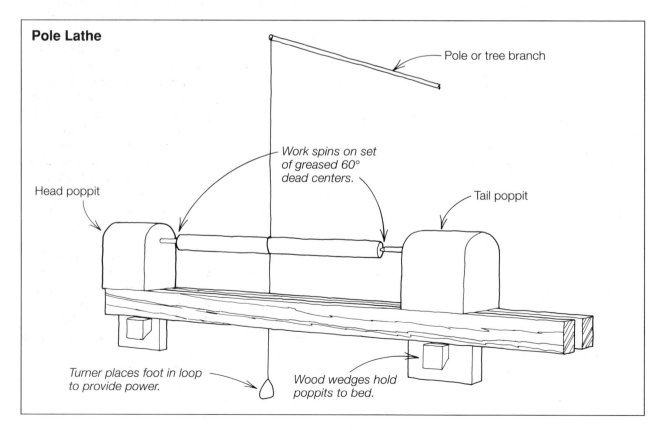

Pole Lathe

Pole or tree branch

Work spins on set of greased 60° dead centers.

Head poppit

Tail poppit

Turner places foot in loop to provide power.

Wood wedges hold poppits to bed.

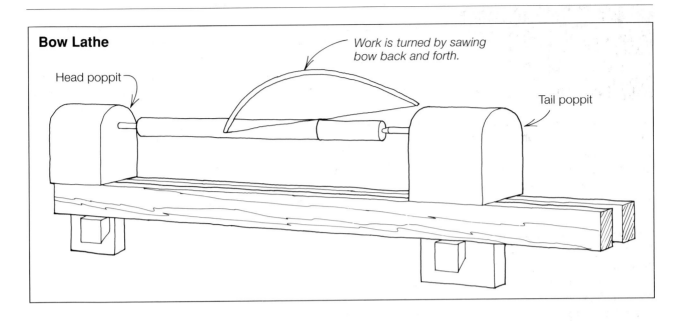

Bow Lathe

Head poppit

Work is turned by sawing bow back and forth.

Tail poppit

controlled with the left. In India and the Far East it's still common to see workers sitting on the ground, using their toes and left hand to guide the tool while they work the bow with their right hand.

Pole and bow lathes were mostly confined to the turning of green wood, that is, freshly fallen timber. Early turners actually worked in the forest, moving their lathes with the receding tree line. Sections of clear trunk would be split, or riven, into suitable turning billets. Such riven wood made very strong spindle turnings because the grain ran the length of the billet.

Although green wood turns with much greater ease than dry stock, pole-lathe turners still used very sharp tools and aggressive shear-cutting techniques—the same techniques we should be using today. Unfortunately, the luxury of today's unlimited power tends to make us lazy. It's all too easy to replace sharp tools and proper techniques with power.

Technological breakthroughs

The first big innovation in lathe design was to replace the sharp 60° point in the left-hand poppit with a live spindle—a spindle set in bearings. By placing a wheel behind the lathe and belting it to the spindle, a much-improved lathe resulted. Such lathes were called "great-wheel lathes" and evolved in Europe where the guild system provided apprentices to crank the wheel. Because the lathe had bearings, much less human effort was wasted to friction. Turners could now concentrate on tool control since they were not distracted by the reverse stroke of the spindle. The live spindle also made faceplate turning without the aid of a tailstock possible.

Improvements in bearings during the 18th century made possible the next major lathe innovation— the development of the treadle lathe. At the same time, the poppit evolved from a wood frame to an iron casting and the headstock was born. A treadle (like that on early sewing machines) was belted to the spindle, and the lathe could be powered by the operator without the aid of an assistant (as was necessary with great-wheel lathes). During this period, lathe beds also evolved from wood planks to cast iron. It was with these innovations that turning first caught on as a hobby.

During the Industrial Revolution the lathe was powered by water, steam, gas engine and electric motor, in about that order. Combined with still further improvements in bearings, better metals and improved manufacturing methods, the modern lathe was born.

The parts of the lathe

All lathes share standard features, although the design, materials and quality vary from model to model. The essential components are the headstock, tailstock, bed, tool base, tool rest, motor and stand.

The headstock

The business end of any lathe—the part that drives the work—is the headstock assembly. The headstock is fixed permanently at the left end of the bed and consists of either a casting, a welded steel body or an extrusion that holds a spindle set in bearings. A pulley on the spindle is connected by a belt to a motor, which is usually mounted below or behind the headstock.

Spindle The spindle, a threaded shaft mounted horizontally, is the heart of the headstock. It accepts the drive centers, face plates and other accessories that hold and power the work (see Chapter 2). Spindles are either hollow or solid and range in size from ½ in. to 1½ in. diameter.

The spindle size you need depends on the type of turning you intend to do. For turning spindles between centers you can get by with a small-diameter spindle. One inch is a common spindle size and is adequate for light-duty work. For heavy-duty faceplate turning and architectural turning you will need at least a 1¼-in. spindle that will not flex under load. Watch out for spindles with odd thread sizes or odd Morse-taper sizes—what may seem like a bargain will be no bargain at all if you can't easily obtain accessories to fit the spindle. The top chart on p. 12 lists the spindle specifications for which you have a good chance of readily finding accessories.

You should give much consideration to the spindle when choosing a lathe. The most important thing to look for is a hollow spindle that is machined to accept Morse-taper accessories. Morse tapers lock in place when inserted into the matching tapered socket in the spindle.

More than any other feature, Morse tapers separate good lathes from bad. Even if your turning needs are very casual, the advantages of Morse tapers are enormous. A Morse-taper socket in the spindle makes for quick and easy mounting of drive centers and a host of other chucking accessories (see the photos on the facing page). Morse tapers lock when driven home and release with an equal opposite force. They're universal, so you're not dependent on the manufacturer for replacement accessories. By contrast, on a lathe that has a solid spindle, all accessories have to be screwed on, which is not only time-consuming but also ties you to the manufacturer.

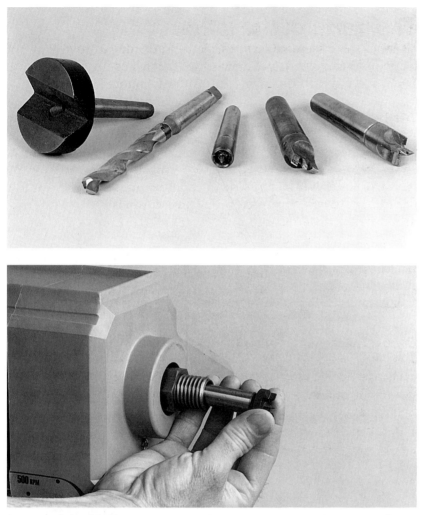

Small Morse tapers can be adapted to larger spindles using Morse-taper sleeves.

Accessories with Morse-taper shanks mount in a matching tapered socket in the headstock spindle. Shown here in the top photo (from left to right) are a crotch center, drill bit, cup center and two drive centers.

Morse tapers are available in sizes #0 through #7. The sizes common to wood lathes are shown in the bottom chart on p. 12. Morse tapers have been widely copied. Other locking tapers include the American Standard Taper, the British Standard Taper, the Brown and Sharps Taper and the Jarno Taper. If you come across a used lathe with a Morse-taper size that does not appear to be standard, *Machinery's Handbook* (Industrial Press, New York, 1988) will be a great help. It lists dimensions for all of the above locking tapers.

Standard Spindle Sizes and Tapers

Spindle thread size	Manufacturer	Morse taper Headstock	Tailstock
⁵⁄₈ in. plain (unthreaded)	Shopsmith	None	#2
¾ in. x 16 TPI*	Sears, Coronet, Record, Beaver	None or #1	None or #1
⁷⁄₈ in. x 14 TPI	Rockwell Homecraft	#1	#1
1 in. x 8 TPI	Delta and many others (most common spindle size)	#2	#2
1 in. x 12 TPI**	Myford	#2	#2
1⅛ in. x 8 TPI	Oliver	#2	#2
1¼ in. x 8 TPI	General	#2	#2
1½ in. x 8 TPI	Conover, Powermatic, Atlas, South Bend	#2 or #3	#2
1½ in. x 6 TPI	Union Graduate (Harrison)	#2	#2

* TPI = threads per inch   ** Whitworth thread (54° flank angle, rather than 60°)

Morse-Taper Sizes

Size	Dia. small end	Dia. large end	Length
#0	.252 in.	.356 in.	2¹¹⁄₃₂ in.
#1	.369 in.	.475 in.	2⁹⁄₁₆ in.
#2	.572 in.	.700 in.	3⅛ in.
#3	.778 in.	.938 in.	3⅞ in.

A further consideration is the height of the spindle above the bed, which dictates the "swing" of the lathe and the diameter of the work that can be turned (see the sidebar on the facing page). At its simplest, swing is double the height of the spindle center over the bed—for example, a lathe with a center height of 6 in. will swing 12 in. You have to be careful of manufacturers' claims here because they often quote the swing over a "gap," which is a short dip in the bed just ahead of the headstock. This gap, which is usually about 2 in. deep, allows you to turn larger-diameter faceplate work in this area. The problem is that when work extends into the gap you can work only on the face of it.

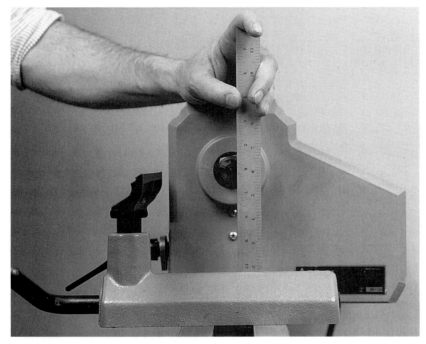

The vertical distance between the spindle and the top of the bed determines the diameter of the work that can be turned on a lathe. In practice, this distance is reduced by the height of the tool base.

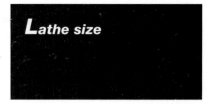

Lathe size is typically specified in three ways, the first two of which are closely related. The first measurement is center height—the distance between the point of a drive center in the spindle and the top of the bed—which determines the diameter of work that the lathe will accommodate. The second measurement is "swing," which is double the center height of the lathe. For standard spindle turning between centers, a center height of 4 in. (yielding a swing of 8 in.) is adequate. For heavy-duty bowl turning, a center height of at least 6 in. is desirable.

The third measurement of lathe size is the maximum distance obtainable between the headstock and tailstock centers. This capacity determines the maximum length of work that can be turned. For spindle turning, 30 in. is the absolute minimum and 36 in. or more is preferable.

Even measuring from the center of the spindle to the bed is not a true measure of capacity. A better yardstick is to measure the distance from the top of the tool base to the center of the spindle. Doubling this will give you the true swing, which is the diameter of work the lathe will swing between centers. Even faceplate turning will generally require placing the tool base under the revolving work.

Bearings   Bearings hold the spindle rigidly in place and allow it to turn with a minimum of friction. They're an important consideration when buying a lathe, though they're a feature that's much harder to judge on cursory examination than, say, the construction method or spindle type.

Historically, lathes have run on plain cast-iron bearings, sleeve bearings and Babbitt bearings, but most lathes made today have rolling-element bearings. These include ball, roller and tapered-roller bearings. Of these, ball bearings (see the photo on p. 14) are by far the most common type used in lathe construction. Each bearing consists of an inner race and an outer race that are separated by a series of steel balls. The opposing ends of the spindle ride on these rings of balls,

Most lathes manufactured today are fitted with ball bearings to hold the spindle. (Photo courtesy of SKF USA, Inc.)

which provide a precise hold and allow the spindle to turn with a minimum of effort. The majority of the power from the motor can now be used for useful work.

Bearings can sometimes be upgraded, which we will discuss later in the section on lathe maintenance (see pp. 142-148).

Outboard turning feature   Because some work will be too large in diameter to swing over the bed, lathe manufacturers often design the headstock so that work can be mounted on the outboard side. Outboard turning is accomplished in two basic ways. One is to put a left-hand thread on the outboard end of the headstock spindle and mount the work so that it faces away from the lathe. The other option is to design the headstock so that it pivots at right angles to the bed.

When work is mounted on the outboard end of the headstock, the swing of the lathe becomes the distance from the center of the headstock spindle to the floor. Although this may sound like an ideal solution for turning large-diameter work, outboard turning presents a number of problems, the greatest of which is speed. Many lathes do not have a low enough speed range to turn anything over 12 in. in diameter. For large-diameter turning you need a bottom speed of 200 rpm to 300 rpm.

Another problem with outboard turning is that there is no place to support the tool rest. You can use a floor-stand rest (usually a tripod stand that holds the rest), but these devices are inherently unstable and even dangerous. Floor-stand rests limit you to light scraping cuts, and you must be ever wary that the stand does not tip into the spinning work. In addition, this method of outboard turning requires a second set of left-hand-threaded face plates and everything is reversed to your normal way of turning. (Delta makes many of their face plates threaded in both directions, which means they can be screwed on either end of the spindle.)

Some lathes that use the outboard end of the spindle for outboard turning have a special tool base attached rigidly to the lathe, which is a much better setup. In effect, this creates a small bowl lathe that is a mirror image of the actual lathe. A bowl lathe is a short lathe designed only for faceplate work—mainly bowls.

The second option for outboard turning—the swing-head design—is the one that I prefer. In a swing-head lathe the headstock pivots at right angles, and the work is turned in front of the lathe (see the photo on the facing page). A special tool base attaches to the base of the headstock and the tool rest fits into this. Although such a setup allows only a limited outboard swing of about 16 in. to 20 in., it's a better

Some lathes have a 'swing-head' design, with a headstock that pivots at right angles to the bed to allow outboard turning in front of the lathe.

arrangement for a number of reasons. First, the diameter of the work is limited to within the low-speed range of the lathe. Second, the tool base is attached rigidly to the lathe headstock, making turning sure and safe. Third, turning is in the same direction and orientation as takes place over the bed. Finally, a second set of left-hand-threaded face plates is not required.

It has been my experience in selling a good many lathes over the years that buyers seem to place unwarranted emphasis on turning outboard. However, outboard turning is something that most people will do only once or twice in their lifetime, if at all. Don't be tunnel-visioned to the outboard feature, ignoring all the other useful features that a lathe should have and that will be used every turning session.

Index head   Some headstocks are fitted with an index head, which is a mechanism that allows the spindle to be locked at equal intervals so that layout or auxiliary operations can be performed. Examples of such applications include laying out a clock face or milling reeds or flutes in a column with a router (see pp. 131-133). The most common setup for indexing is a series of holes drilled in the back of the head-stock drive pulley (see the photo on p. 5), which is mounted on the spindle. A pin in the headstock casting slides into the appropriate hole and locks the spindle in place. Common hole patterns are 12, 24 and 60. I like the 24-stop configuration because it allows me to divide the circumference of a workpiece into eight equal parts (an octagon is a common period-furniture shape).

Indexing is a feature that may or may not be of value to you. I have spoken to many turners who have never used the index head. For certain types of period-furniture turning, such as fluted legs, it is essential. If you are considering a dandy lathe at a bargain price but it lacks indexing, buy it anyway. An index head can be added later if you need it. There are several after-market chucks that incorporate the feature, or you can rig something up yourself. Note that the index head should not be used as a spindle lock for removing faceplates because doing so may bend the indexing stop. Most lathes have other provisions for locking the spindle for faceplate removal.

Motors, belts and pulleys

Almost all woodworking lathes are supplied with a single-phase induction motor. The motor typically mounts inside the stand or at the back of the headstock and is connected to a pulley on the spindle by a belt. For small lathes, ½ hp is adequate, whereas bigger machines require 1 hp or even 1½ hp. Machines imported from Asia frequently have power specifications on the motor nameplate that are optimistic. Often such machines are otherwise quite serviceable, so the best course is to replace the anemic motor with a U.S. model.

Increasingly, manufacturers are putting DC (direct current) motors with solid-state controllers on lathes. Today's solid-state circuitry allows controllers that efficiently make DC current from ordinary single-phase household current. This makes it possible simply to dial a speed, which is much more convenient than having to move the belt by hand to change speed. Such a controller cannot be used with a standard induction motor. The one drawback to the DC motor is its cost.

Belts and pulleys   The original drive system for connecting lathes to the power source was a flat leather belt. A three- or four-step set of matched pulleys would give a good range of speeds for the turner. Although flat leather belts gave very constant speed with no surging, they tended to slip and hence wasted power.

Most lathes made in recent times use V-belts for power transmission. V-belts drive positively because greater tension on the belt causes it to wedge tighter in the pulley groove. An additional advantage of V-belts is that manufacturers can provide variable speed by installing a variable-width pulley set (shown on the facing page). A mechanical control adjusts the width of the drive pulley, which effectively changes the diameter and the speed. Moving the two halves of the drive pulley apart decreases the diameter (and decreases the speed); squeezing the halves back together does the reverse. The mating pulley on the headstock is similarly split, but spring loaded so it automatically adjusts to the drive pulley. This setup gives a wide range of infinitely variable speeds.

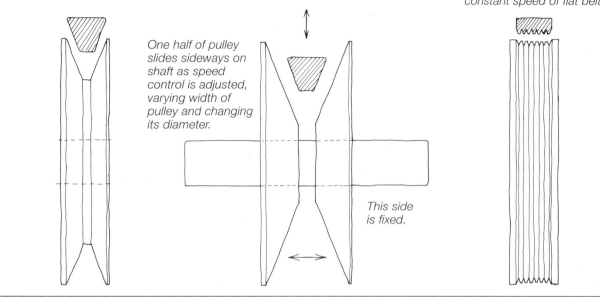

Drive Pulley Systems

V-belt and pulley

V-belt wedges in pulley, giving positive drive.

Variable speed V-belt

Belt rides up and down as diameter of pulley changes.

Poly V-belt

Belt combines positive drive of standard V-belt with constant speed of flat belt.

One half of pulley slides sideways on shaft as speed control is adjusted, varying width of pulley and changing its diameter.

This side is fixed.

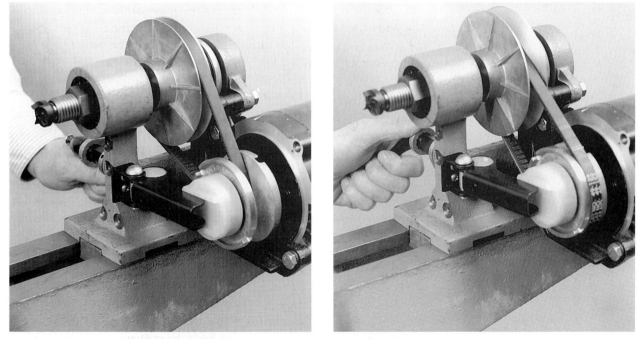

Turning speed can be adjusted at the touch of a handle on a lathe fitted with a variable-width pulley set. Shown here is the Delta Vari Drive system, adjusted for low speed (left) and high speed (right).

A recent innovation is the poly V-belt, which is a flat rubber belt with a series of small V-ribs machined on the inside surface. This design gives the belt the positive drive characteristics of a V-belt with the constant velocity of a flat leather belt. Many newer lathes run on poly V-belts.

The tailstock

The tailstock assembly is comprised of the main casting, a spindle (or ram), a spindle-locking lever, a handwheel and a mechanism to secure the unit to the lathe bed. Whereas the headstock is stationary, the tailstock can be slid along the bed to accommodate work of varying length. It is locked at the desired distance from the headstock.

The advantages of a good tailstock should not be overlooked, because it does much more than just hold a center. As with the headstock spindle, the tailstock spindle should be machined to accept Morse-taper accessories. Look for a spindle equipped with a #1 or a #2 Morse taper. The tailstock spindle sometimes runs a bit smaller than the headstock spindle; for example, if the headstock spindle is $1\frac{1}{2}$ in. in diameter, the tailstock spindle is typically 1 in.

An important aspect of tailstock design is spindle travel—the amount the spindle can be moved when the tailstock is locked to the bed. Lathes typically have about $2\frac{1}{2}$ in. of spindle travel, which is adequate for most applications. I prefer to work with a tailstock spindle that can move as much as possible, because the tailstock itself doesn't have to be moved as often.

The tailstock spindle is advanced and withdrawn by a handwheel. A lever on top of the tailstock locks the spindle in place and prevents it from drifting during turning operations. The traditional setup is for the outside of the spindle to be left-hand threaded, and the handwheel, which is no more than a large nut, winds it back and forth (see the photo at left, facing page). By making the thread left-handed, the spindle advances when the handwheel is turned clockwise, which is normal to our way of thinking. This design is usually used on cheaper lathes, although it is sometimes also found on very expensive ones. Accessories are ejected by inserting a knockout bar through the spindle.

A more elegant arrangement is a self-ejecting spindle. The inside of the spindle is left-hand threaded, and a long left-hand screw extends from the handwheel into it (photo at right, facing page). Turning the wheel to the right advances the spindle, while turning it left withdraws it. As the spindle is retracted all the way rearward, the screw bumps the Morse taper in the spindle and ejects it. A crank handle is often added to the handwheel so that the spindle can be moved quickly. Occasion-

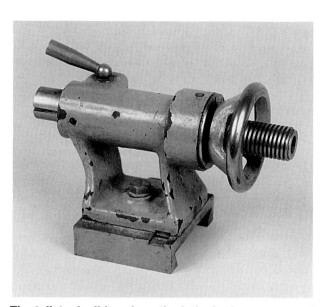

The tailstock slides along the lathe bed to accommodate work of varying length. There are two basic designs: one (left), where the Morse taper is removed by inserting a knockout bar through the spindle; the other (right), here viewed from the back of the lathe, where the taper self-ejects when the spindle is withdrawn all the way. (Photo at right courtesy of Delta)

ally a taper is too short to eject, so it is always good to check any new accessory by lightly inserting it and running the spindle rearward to see if it ejects.

The tailstock must lock securely to the bed and not move while you're turning. There are a variety of locking mechanisms, ranging from a stud running down between the bed rails with a plate and a nut, to complicated cams. The main thing to look for is a good positive lock that will hold the tailstock without its drifting backward when you apply pressure to the work with the handwheel.

Center alignment   When you buy a new lathe, it's a good idea to check that the tailstock aligns with the headstock. (This test will also check the truth of the bed.) The best gauge for testing center alignment is a pair of 60° dead centers (see p. 37), but any set of Morse-taper accessories that come to a point at the center will work. Simply put one center in the tailstock and one center in the headstock and slide the tailstock forward until the two points touch. The centers should align perfectly.

Center alignment is important in faceplate work but relatively unimportant for spindle turning. For faceplate work it is often necessary to utilize the tailstock for support, or to perform an ancillary operation such as drilling. Since the faceplate is screwed securely on the spindle, the tailstock must be in perfect center alignment with it. For spindle work, the turner shapes the turning by eye relative to the centerline of the turning itself. Although reasonable center alignment is advantageous (if for no other reason than that the tool rest aligns with the work), center alignment could vary by ⅛ in. or more on a 15-in. spindle. The longer the turning, the more out of alignment the two centers could be.

The bed

The lathe bed supports the headstock, tailstock and tool-rest assembly and is in turn supported by a stand. The earliest lathe beds were no more than two wood planks, and wood is still used on some modern lathes. Wood has much to recommend itself as a bed material—it is relatively cheap, readily available, absorbs vibration and can yield a lathe of any desired length between centers. The springiness of a timber bed has shock-absorbing characteristics unmatched by metal.

Starting in the 18th century, cast-iron lathe beds began to displace wood. Cast iron is a good bed material because it is stable and has excellent vibration-damping characteristics. The casting process allows beds of intricate design to be made. In an iron bed each of the wood planks is replaced by a strip, or rib, which is called a "way." The bed ways are usually between 1 in. and 1½ in. apart.

Although structural steel does not have the damping ability of cast iron, it still makes a good solid bed. Steel also makes possible longer beds at reasonable cost. You can even make a "stretched" structural steel bed by obtaining lengths of matching steel from a steel fabricator.

I've seen one lathe with a bed made from aluminum extrusions. Extrusions don't have much to recommend themselves as a bed material for anything but a miniature lathe, so I would avoid them on a full-sized lathe.

The main things to look for in a bed are rigidity and workmanship. The ways should have a smooth surface, and the distance between them should be constant. Make sure the tailstock and tool base slide easily but lock solid where you put them. Test the truth of the bed by checking the alignment of the headstock and tailstock (see p. 19).

The tool rest

What we tend to think of as the tool rest is actually composed of two parts—the tool-base assembly and the tool rest itself. The tool base, which supports the tool rest, attaches to the bed of the lathe and can be slid to any point between the headstock and the tailstock. The base also moves in and out so that the tool rest can be positioned right next to the workpiece. Desirable features in a tool base include ease of movement, rigidity and a low profile. The latter feature is important because the height of the base affects the swing of the lathe (see pp. 12-13). For each $\frac{1}{8}$ in. the tool-base height is reduced we are rewarded with an extra $\frac{1}{4}$ in. of swing.

The tool base must lock down securely and not slide under load. The hold-down/locking mechanisms range from wedges under the bed that are pounded snug with a mallet on classic wood-bed machines, to a simple nut and bolt that are tightened with a wrench on economy lathes, to complicated lever-operated cam mechanisms on full-featured machines. With each level of sophistication comes commensurate increases in price. When choosing a lathe, the best course is to try the tool base and see how it operates. Move it to a variety of angles and positions, lock it in place, grab it with both hands and see if you can move it. Don't be afraid to throw some body weight into this exercise.

The tool rest provides a fulcrum point for support and control of tools during turning. The rest mounts in the tool base and is adjustable to any height and angle. A locking mechanism (usually a simple knob and stud, sometimes a cam) secures the rest in the tool base. The front surface of the rest should have sufficient slope so that any tool will contact only the top edge in any turning operation. The tool rest should

The tool-base assembly should lock securely to the bed and slide freely for easy adjustment.

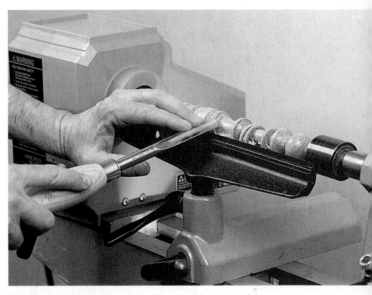

The tool rest clamps into the tool base and is adjustable to any height and angle.

be of solid construction—structural steel performs as well as cast iron, and you can also use wood. Tool rests come in standard lengths of 6 in., 12 in., 18 in. and 36 in. Sometimes the longer rests require two tool bases. For special turning situations, you can have a local welder fabricate a longer rest from structural steel, or you can make your own full-length tool rest out of wood (see pp. 154-156).

The stand

When choosing a lathe, it's important to look for a solid stand that will prevent the lathe from jumping around under full load. Nineteenth- and early 20th-century lathes typically had heavy cast-iron legs (weighing as much as 300 lb.) that minimized vibration. The legs were usually bolted to the end of the bed, which made for a freestanding machine that you could stand close to without stubbing your toes.

In this century, cast-iron legs have largely been replaced by stamped-sheet-metal stands. By using angle and box sections, a serviceable stand can be fabricated from light-gauge material. Such stands are in-expensive to manufacture, cut down on shipping weight and, if shipped knocked down, save on shipping volume. A well-designed sheet-metal stand can be very good indeed, whereas a poorly designed stand can impair the performance of an otherwise good lathe.

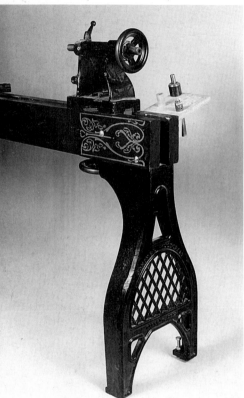

Heavy cast-iron legs provide a rock-solid stand for a lathe.

A shopmade plywood box stand filled with sand provides solid support for the lathe and minimizes vibration.

Some economy lathes are sold with the stand as an option. These stands are invariably of poor quality, and you're much better off building your own stand. Building plywood box sections and filling them with sand will give you a base that soaks up vibration and cuts down on lathe noise. The plywood is stronger and more rigid than any stamped-steel stand. You can also add a shopmade stand to a quality lathe—I built my favorite lathe (shown on the facing page) with triangular plywood box legs, each filled with 100 lb. of sand.

Avoid shelves and drawers under your lathe. They tend to fill with chips and collect dust. I prefer a lathe with legs on either end rather than a box underneath, because sweeping and shoveling chips is much easier with this design.

Setting up a lathe

Setting up a lathe involves more than just shoehorning the machine into an available space in the workshop. You need to consider workflow, machine placement, chip removal, ventilation, electrical service, lighting and tool storage. Taking time to plan things before you install the lathe will save hours, days, even months in increased production time down the road.

Workflow

The lathe should be placed in such a way that work can flow naturally to and from other machines in the shop. Billets for spindle turning are often jointed and planed square. They are then cut to length on a table saw or radial-arm saw. Keeping this flow in mind when placing the lathe will save unnecessary trips across the workshop. Access to the bandsaw, which is often used to round up faceplate work before it is mounted in the lathe, may be important depending on your work. And whatever type of turning you do, it's a good idea to mount the grinder close to the lathe so you won't have far to walk to sharpen your tools.

Machine placement

Most people tend to put a lathe against a wall, but I think that placing it at right angles or at a 45° angle to a wall makes more sense. You still have the wall for tool racks, but lathe access is much better. And if your lathe has a sheet-metal box-type stand you need enough room in back of it to sweep, since more than half the chips will accumulate there. Putting a lathe against a wood or metal post is another good option. Electrical outlets, lights and tool racks can be mounted on the post, turning what might otherwise be a dead area into useful space.

Many lathes today are built with sheet-metal stands. Shown here is the General 260. (Photo courtesy of General Mfg.).

Dolling out the shop

Many years ago I made a scale drawing of my shop. I included every electrical outlet and window on my plan, and drew dotted squares on the floor to represent the lights that hung overhead. Then, on a separate sheet of paper, I drew to scale the outside footprint of each machine. I cut out the machines and placed them on the plan, gluing them down when I found their ideal location. I even cut out a scale 4x8 sheet of plywood to check clearances around machines.

I learned the technique from my father, who calls it "dolling out the shop," because of its similarity to cutting out the shapes of clothes for paper dolls. Dolling out your shop is good practice and will allow you to place your lathe where it will not interfere with workflow but will have good access to light, power and material. It's sure easier to move squares of paper than 500-lb. machines.

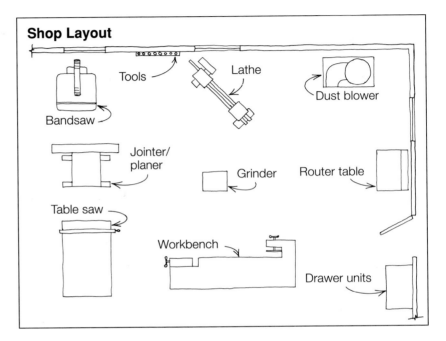

Shop Layout

Tools · Lathe · Dust blower · Bandsaw · Jointer/planer · Grinder · Router table · Table saw · Workbench · Drawer units

Once you've actually positioned your lathe, it needs to be leveled. Test for level parallel to and across the bed ways using a standard builder's level. If you need to level the stand, use wood shims rather than metal because wood is more resilient. A thin sheet of industrial rubber under each leg can help reduce vibration. I've used scrap truck inner tube successfully, cementing the tube to a 3-in. or 4-in. square of ½-in. plywood and placing a square under each corner of the machine. I place additional shims of ⅛-in. Masonite on top of the base plywood shim for fine adjustment.

Now is a good time to consider machine height. Most lathes seem a little low to me, and I can only attribute this to the fact that human stature has increased markedly this century. A good rule of thumb is to have the spindle centerline at elbow height, or just a touch higher. For most people this height is between 40 in. and 44 in. To raise the height of the lathe, add 4x4 blocks with rubber glued to the underside. Of course, the best option is to build your own stand so that the working height is exactly right for you.

For normal spindle turning a lathe need not be bolted to the floor. In fact, I prefer the flexibility that leaving it unbolted allows—if my lathe needs to be moved for some reason, it's an easy matter, and I don't have to drill holes in my shop floor. If I need to weigh the machine down for heavier turning I drape sand bags over the legs.

Chip removal and ventilation

A lathe generates a good deal of mess, and more than partial chip extraction with a dust-collection system is difficult. If your shop has a dust-collection system, it's a good idea to locate a pickup port near the lathe. By placing a hose as close as possible to the work, much of the dust from sanding can be vacuumed away. I've seen one shop where a short length of flexible metal automotive exhaust pipe emanated from the pickup port. Like a gooseneck lamp, this pipe could be arranged for maximum debris removal. You can also wheel portable dust blowers to the lathe and clamp a suitable wood bracket to the lathe to hold the pickup hose close to the work.

If you don't have a dust-collection system, being able to open doors and windows will help. In good weather, placing an exhaust fan in the window near your lathe will carry most of the dust outside, which will not only make a turning session more enjoyable but will also be better for your health. For more on dust protection, see the safety section below.

Electrical service

It's important to have good access to electrical outlets at your lathe. Not only should there be an outlet for the lathe itself, but there should also be enough 120-volt outlets for portable power tools that will be used with the lathe such as electric drills, sanders and routers. Avoid running on extension cords because long cords can cause power loss, which will result in lower voltage at the machine. This in turn will cause the motor to run hotter. Although this may not be enough to trip the breaker or blow a fuse, it can shorten the life of the motor. It will also be noticeable in less power and more frequent stalling of the machine. The cord can also trip you.

Make sure that you have properly grounded outlets that meet your local electrical building codes. Electrical codes vary from region to region, so it's difficult to state what will be acceptable in your locality. Minimum standards for an outlet are that it should be a properly grounded, fused circuit with wire gauge adequate for the required amperage. Some localities may require additional measures, such as running wires in conduit.

If you have an electrician run a new circuit, be sure to install GFCI (Ground Fault Circuit Interrupter) breakers at the same time. GFCI breakers are code in most states for bathrooms, basements and garages. They sense any problem in grounding and break the circuit, saving countless lives. They are well worth the money. If you find that your lathe is tripping the GFCI breaker constantly, there's a problem with your lathe. Get it fixed!

If possible, run your lathe on 220-volt current rather than 110-volt. Your motor will start more quickly and overcome turning resistance more easily. It will also be slightly cheaper to operate the motor on the higher voltage. While it is tempting to put a 10-ft. or 15-ft. lead on your motor, it's not a good idea. The plug at the end of the cord provides a second disconnect should the switch fail or if it is unsafe to get to the switch. Also it is imperative to unplug the machine during certain operations such as maintenance. Local code often specifies that this plug/disconnect should be no more than 6 ft. from the machine.

If you're at all uncertain about electrical matters, hire a competent licensed electrician to do any wiring you need in your shop.

Lighting

The importance of good lighting at the lathe cannot be overemphasized. I prefer to work by natural light, so the lathes I work on most often are near windows. Natural light is especially helpful when matching stains and colors. Fluorescent lighting tends to be very cold, so I opt for full-spectrum tubes that more closely mimic sunlight. When I ran a shop, I always felt that the warmer light gave people a better attitude, and there have been some studies to support this opinion.

Although good general lighting is all that is necessary, it may be useful also to attach a work lamp to the lathe. Sophisticated models with long articulated arms are available at discount stores. Such a light will be helpful for fine detail work or for seeing inside hollow work such as bowls.

Tool storage

Tool storage around a lathe can present a real problem. Shelves or drawers under the lathe fill with chips. Tool racks attached to the front of the lathe tend to get in the way. Without a tool rack of some sort, you'll end up balancing three tools on the bed and one will invariably fall off, point first. After I'd made hundreds of trips to the grinder to fix such mishaps, master woodturner Palmer Sharpless showed me a simple rack that fits between the bed ways. It supports a working complement of three to five tools and can be moved anywhere along the bed with the needs of the job.

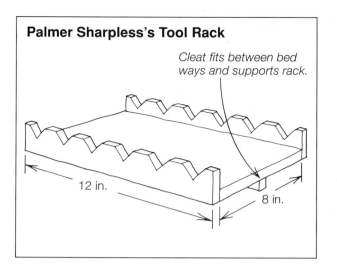

Palmer Sharpless's Tool Rack

Cleat fits between bed ways and supports rack.

12 in.

8 in.

Master turner Joe Herrmann demonstrates a freestanding tool rack.

For the rest of your tools, there are several options. One is to mount a tool rack on the wall or post near your lathe. A serviceable rack can be made quickly by drilling holes of the appropriate diameter in a strip of wood, then affixing it to the wall. Design it with minimal horizontal surfaces to collect dust. My friend Dave Hout uses a very simple free-standing rack he made himself. Tools stand vertically in the rack, and the handles are at just the right height for your hand when your arm is naturally at your side. Dave places the rack slightly behind him and has to make only a half-turn to reach the necessary tool. The rack is away from the worst chip fallout and can be moved easily for sweeping.

Safety

The lathe enjoys a fairly good safety record, but it's important not to take a cavalier approach to the machine. Unlike saws and jointers, the lathe doesn't have moving parts that will sever fingers, but turning accidents, sometimes fatal, can and do happen. As with any tool, knowledge of the potential dangers will help ensure safer operation. The main areas of concern are "flyers" (work flying out of, or coming apart in, the lathe); speed, which is closely related to flyers; clothing, jewelry and hair becoming entangled in the spinning work; electrical shock; eye injuries; and dust inhalation. Let's take a look at each of these areas in turn.

• Make sure the lathe is properly grounded and meets local electrical codes.

• Make sure the work is securely mounted in the lathe.

• Check for any defects in the wood you are planning to turn.

• Always start the lathe at an appropriate speed.

• Never touch or move the belt while the lathe is running, and never run the lathe without the belt cover in place.

• Never stick your fingers in the spindle while the lathe is running.

• When mounting a new workpiece, check that the tool rest clears the work and that the rest is securely locked in position before starting the lathe.

• Listen for unusual sounds coming from the lathe—they can indicate that something is wrong.

• Always unplug the lathe while performing maintenance or repairs.

• Use the correct tools for the job—roughing gouges and skew chisels should not be used for faceplate turning.

• Always work with tools that are sharp.

• Wear appropriate safety equipment for eye and lung protection, and clothes without dangling ends.

• Take frequent breaks, especially when doing repetitive work where your mind may drift.

Flyers and speed

Work flying out of the lathe and glued-up work flying apart in the lathe constitute by far the biggest dangers in turning. In a few rare instances, flying work has even caused death—usually when the operator is hit in the head. Such accidents can almost always be traced back to starting the lathe at too high a speed for the turning operation. Having taught hundreds of people to turn, I've observed that most students approach the lathe with their mind totally fixed on the problems of producing a usable turning. Speed is the last thing on their mind, and it should be the first.

You need to work out a routine that will prevent flyers. Form the habit of returning your lathe to its lowest speed at the end of every turning session. Unplugging it at this time and draping the plug across the bed is a great reminder. Make speed concerns the foremost thought in your mind as you approach the lathe, and setting the appropriate speed the first order of business when chucking up work. Rotate the work by hand to make sure that it clears the tool rest before you turn the lathe on. Finally, if you're the least unsure, stand to the left of the lathe when you turn it on. If the work is going to fly, you're out of the line of fire.

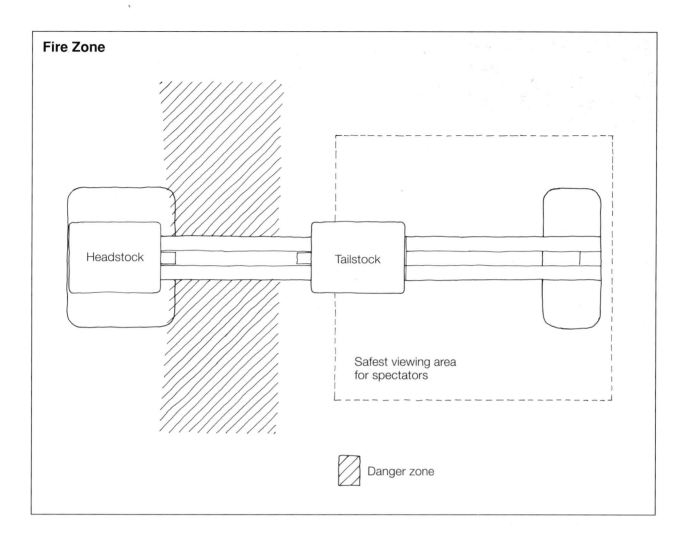

Fire Zone

Headstock

Tailstock

Safest viewing area
for spectators

Danger zone

The tool rest provides some protection to the operator, since it directs a high percentage of the flyers to the back of the lathe, but you also need to protect any observers in your shop. Flyers tend to travel at right angles to the headstock spindle, so don't let spectators stand in the area 90° to the spinning work. The best place for viewers to stand is around the tailstock (see the drawing above). Warning others in the shop when you first start the lathe after mounting work will do much to prevent accidents.

Appropriate turning speed is a difficult thing to specify. As with driving a car, you can negotiate higher speeds as you gain experience, but for beginners it's always best to err on the side of low speed. Except for miniature work, turning need never take place at a speed higher than 2,000 rpm. Sanding is best done at the final turning speed and does not, as some sources recommend, require higher speeds.

For turning spindles up to 2½ in. in diameter, which is to say standard furniture spindles, a roughing speed of about 1,100 rpm and a finishing speed of about 1,700 rpm are appropriate. The experienced turner will be able to do the entire operation at the higher speed as long as the work is well centered to start with.

Faceplate turning is more prone to flyers because of the greater diameter of the work and the greater difficulty in centering. For work up to 10 in. in diameter, 600 rpm to 800 rpm is a good roughing speed; 1,100 rpm is an appropriate finishing speed. Face work need never be done at a speed greater than 1,100 rpm. For large-diameter face work, speeds as low as 200 rpm may be necessary.

Chucking work correctly in the lathe is an important part of the safety equation. Proper mounting of work is imperative and will be covered in detail in Chapter 2.

Clothing, hair and jewelry

It's good shop practice to roll up your sleeves, restrain long hair and remove jewelry. A suit and tie are not appropriate for turning. You want dress that is devoid of any dangling ends that may become entangled in the lathe. Similarly, when applying finish to a piece, never use a rag larger than about 2 in. square—a small rag will be pulled from your fingers whereas a larger one can drag them with it. Finally, always wear sturdy shoes when turning to provide protection against dropped tools or workpieces.

Electrical safety

As well as making sure that the lathe is properly grounded and that your electrical service meets local codes (see pp. 25-26), there are some other electrical safety concerns. Always unplug the motor while carrying out lathe maintenance, repairs or moving the machine. In the event of a power interruption, turn your lathe off before investigating the problem. If power interruptions are a common problem, you may want to equip your lathe with a magnetic starting switch, which will require restarting once power is restored.

Eye and dust protection

Some sort of eye protection is essential when operating a lathe. A minimum is a pair of shatterproof eye glasses, preferably with side shields. For some types of work, such as turning wood with bark still on it or exceptionally splintery material, a full face shield should be worn.

Equally important is to protect yourself from dust. Wood dust, especially from tropical species, can be quite toxic and even carcinogenic. A paper dust mask, like those worn in automotive body shops, is a minimum requirement. Better protection is afforded by a respirator, which has replaceable cartridge-type filters and looks like a military gas mask. Respirators offer good dust protection, but they're hot and tiring to wear because you're doing the air pumping with your lungs. They also are a problem for turners who have beards because of the difficulty of obtaining a tight seal.

The best form of protection for both the eyes and the lungs is an air helmet. Air helmets offer the safety of a full face shield and hard hat with excellent dust protection that does not tax your respiratory system. They have a battery-powered motor that pumps air into the helmet, which provides positive air pressure inside the shield, excluding dust and preventing fogging. Since the motor is doing the pumping, not your lungs, breathing is much easier than with a respirator. Although some air helmets filter only dust, others also filter organic vapors from glues and finishing products. Air helmets cost a lot more than other types of dust protectors (as much as $350), but if you do much woodworking they're well worth the price.

Air helmets (this one is the Airstream helmet made by Racal) provide excellent protection against dust and eye injuries.

CHAPTER 2
Holding the Work

Now that you have your lathe set up and running, it's time to think about turning something. But first you need a way to hold the work in the lathe. I've always maintained that I can turn anything, given a way to mount it in my lathe. This is where chucking comes in. Technically, a chuck is any device that holds work in the lathe—it can be a set of centers, a faceplate, an elaborately manufactured jaw-type chuck or a simple shopmade glue block.

Understanding the difference between spindle turning and faceplate turning is central to the concept of chucking. In spindle turning, the grain of the wood being turned runs between the centers of the lathe, that is, parallel to the axis of the lathe. In faceplate turning, the grain of the work runs at right angles to the axis of the lathe (see the drawings on p. 34). Although we commonly associate turning between centers with spindle turning, it's possible to hold work this way and yet be faceplate turning. Similarly, it's possible to have something screwed onto a faceplate and still be spindle turning. The screws in this case would be into the end grain of the wood. The important thing to remember is that the orientation of the grain, not how the work is held, dictates the type of turning. Each type of work also requires different tools and turning techniques, as we shall see in Chapters 3 and 4.

Work can be held in the lathe between centers, on a faceplate or using a special-purpose chuck such as the jam chuck shown here.

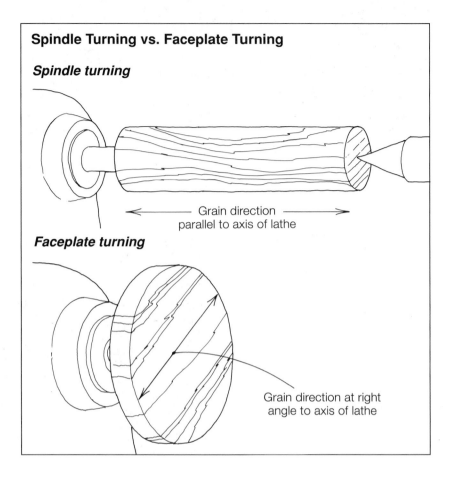

Spindle Turning vs. Faceplate Turning

Spindle turning

Grain direction
parallel to axis of lathe

Faceplate turning

Grain direction at right
angle to axis of lathe

Centers

The oldest and simplest way to hold work in the lathe is between a set of centers, one mounted in the headstock and the other in the tailstock. Most spindle work is held this way. Centers are a fast and reliable way to mount work, and they allow unlimited chucking and unchucking, which is an advantage for trial fitting of turned furniture parts, or to allow stains and finishes to dry between lathe operations.

Drive centers

The drive center, or spur center, mounts in the headstock spindle. It both holds the work and transmits power to it. The shaft of the center is a Morse taper that fits in a matching socket in the spindle. The business end of the center is a small central point surrounded by spurs or tines. The central point should protrude $\frac{1}{16}$ in. to $\frac{1}{8}$ in. beyond the face of the tines to ensure centering of the work at the desired point before the tines bite in. On better drive centers, the central point is removable and/or adjustable for the amount it stands proud of the tines.

Drive centers with two or four spurs mount in the headstock. Two-spur centers (shown above) provide the surest grip on work that doesn't have a square-cut end.

Drive centers are sold in both two-spur and four-spur models. Four-spur centers are more common, but my preference is the two-spur variety (see the top photo above and the drawing on p. 36). It drives as well as the four-spur and can be oriented to give positive drive no matter what the contour of the end of the turning billet. A four-spur center, on the other hand, can bite securely only if the end of the work is square. If the surface is irregular, the four-spur center will drive on only one tine, which can cause the work to go off center and even kick out of the lathe in extreme cases. If your lathe comes with a four-spur center, you can easily modify it by grinding two of the tines away.

Each tine of a spur center comes to a chisel edge. These edges must not be in line with each other or the center will become a wedge and split the work. If the tines become dull or damaged they can be ground back to a chisel edge (grind on the bevel side only). You should also keep the central point sharp; if it is removable, mount it in a cordless drill and simply touch it to a running grinder.

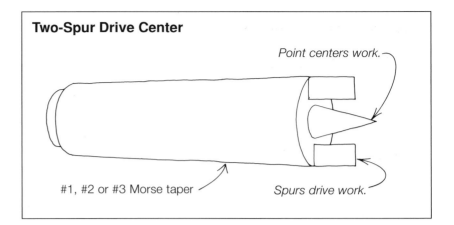

Two-Spur Drive Center

Point centers work.

#1, #2 or #3 Morse taper

Spurs drive work.

It's not necessary to pound the center into the work or to saw lines in the end of the billet, as some turners recommend, to achieve positive drive. Pressure from the tailstock is sufficient to drive the tines into the work. Even on small lathes there is tremendous mechanical advantage in the screw-thread mechanism of the tailstock handwheel.

It's a good idea to grind a nick on the outer radial surface of one of the tines. Whenever you remove work from the lathe but plan to rechuck it, make a pencil mark on the workpiece next to the nick so you can reposition it accurately. With wear, sharpening and mishaps such as drops on concrete, each tine gets to be a different length. Unless the work is repositioned on the drive center exactly the way it was removed, perfect centering will be difficult. Your pencil mark and nick make rechucking a simple matter.

Standard drive centers are available in Morse-taper sizes #1, #2 and #3. If you plan to turn miniature work such as doll-house furniture, a standard drive center is too large and will get in the way. The solution is to buy a mini drive center, which is simply a miniaturized drive center with an outside diameter between ⅜ in. and ½ in.

Tailstock centers

The tailstock center, which mounts in the tailstock spindle, centers the work and exerts force through itself to the drive center in the headstock. It also gives radial support to the work, thereby holding it in the lathe. As with drive centers, the tailstock center has a Morse-taper shaft, but the business end is quite different.

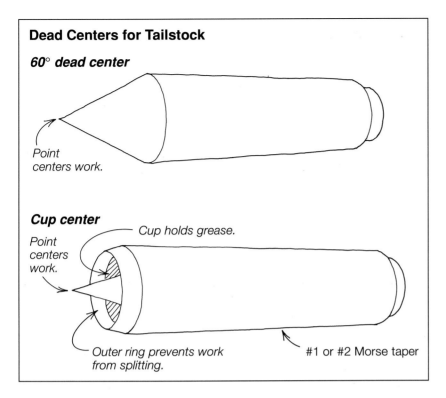

Dead Centers for Tailstock

60° dead center

Point centers work.

Cup center

Cup holds grease.

Point centers work.

Outer ring prevents work from splitting.

#1 or #2 Morse taper

There are two types of tailstock centers: dead centers and live centers. The dead center is the traditional design and consists of a simple pivot bearing on which the work rotates. The end that bites into the work is either a 60° point or a cup center, which is a small center point surrounded by a raised ring (see the drawing above). Dead centers are inexpensive, and many lathes still come with a dead center in the standard accessory kit. Because the center is stationary, it needs to be lubricated to reduce friction and heat buildup from the rotating workpiece. Any grease will do as a lubricant—I once used butter from a high school cafeteria to get me through a demonstration. No matter what the lubricant, some burning is to be expected with a dead center.

Live centers are a great improvement on dead centers because the center point is mounted on a ball bearing and rotates with the spinning work, eliminating the need for lubrication and the risk of burning. In addition, you can exert much greater force on the work with a live center, which means that the work is held more securely. The drawback to live centers is, of course, their higher price.

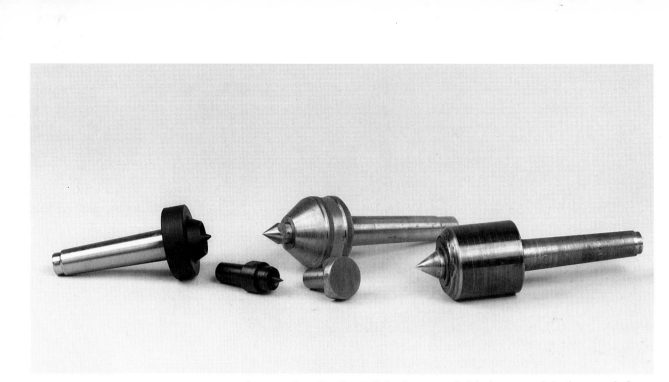

Live centers for the tailstock are available in several designs and sizes. Shown here are the Delta economy cup center (left), the Delta multipurpose center with interchangeable inserts (middle) and the Conover multipurpose center with a 60° point installed (right).

Better live centers are sold with two or three interchangeable points. The 60° point and cup center are standard designs, and some live centers also come with a third flat-faced insert (see the photo above), which is used for special tasks such as holding a bowl in a jam chuck or metal spinning.

The idea behind the cup center is that the outside ring prevents the work from splitting (and holds grease). In my experience, a 60° point has no greater tendency to split work than a cup point. What's more, it holds in a much smaller area, which allows you to turn right up to the point, and wears much better in service. For these reasons, the 60° point is the only point I give my students. You can often get 60° live centers from metalworking supply houses at bargain prices. Even though these centers are designed for metalworking lathes, they work fine for woodturning.

Faceplates

Faceplates are used to hold work that can't be supported (or that you don't want to support) by a tailstock. Since this situation encompasses most faceplate work, the type of turning has been named for the chucking method. As mentioned previously, however, it's the orientation of the grain that makes it face work, not how the work is held.

A faceplate is simply a metal disc with a threaded hub that screws onto the headstock spindle. A circle (or circles) of holes around the periphery allows work to be fastened to the plate with screws. Today, many faceplates are made from cast aluminum, which works fine for most operations but is not suitable for large-diameter and/or heavy work. For heavy-duty faceplate turning there is no substitute for cast iron or steel.

Faceplates are available in various diameters depending on the lathe manufacturer—3 in., 6 in. and 9 in. are common sizes. Most woodworkers seem to think that they need a large faceplate, but for the vast majority of your work the 3-in. plate (often known as a "bowl chuck") will serve you much better. The base of a knob or a bowl should be about one-third the widest dimension. With the work mounted on a 6-in. faceplate it's next to impossible to turn the base (unless the work is more than 18 in. in diameter). I recommend that you buy four or five

Faceplates are used to mount flat work in the headstock. The three stacked faceplates are cast iron; the other two are aluminum alloy (front) and steel (right).

3-in. faceplates so you don't have to mount and unmount them all the time (see p. 51). You'll need a larger faceplate only if you plan to turn large-diameter, heavy work.

Faceplates are manufactured to fit standard spindle sizes (see the chart on p. 12). If you have a lathe with an oddball spindle size, you can make your own faceplate—provided you can find a nut that fits the spindle. Have an industrial weld shop weld a large, heavy, flat washer to the nut. Drill and countersink evenly spaced screw holes around the periphery of the washer. You can use the lathe's indexing mechanism (see pp. 15-16) to lay out the holes.

Most faceplates have a flat surface, but the better models have a ledge around the outer edge. The ledge allows the plate to seat flat on uneven surfaces much better. If you have flat aluminum-alloy faceplates, you can modify them yourself by using a sharp turning scraper to turn a shallow recess in the face of the plate (see the photo on the facing page).

Face work flying off of faceplates presents the greatest safety hazard in turning (see p. 30). It is imperative to ensure that your work is securely screwed to the faceplate before you begin turning. In the past, wood screws were used for this purpose, but the sheet-metal screws available today provide a much surer hold. Sheet-metal screws have a straight body and 45° thread profile that bites into wood much better than wood screws. They are also mildly heat treated, which gives them added strength and toughness.

As a minimum, you should use #10 sheet-metal screws to secure work to the faceplate. I use two sizes: #12 x 1 in. for the lion's share of my work and #12 x 1½ in. when extra surety is needed. Under no circumstances should you use drywall screws—they're hard and brittle and so might snap under load.

Most bowl chucks have only three holes around the circumference. It's a good idea to drill and countersink an extra hole between each of the originals for a total of six. This allows you to use six screws in demanding situations, thereby greatly increasing the holding power of the faceplate.

Turning a shallow recess in an aluminum-alloy faceplate helps it seat better on uneven surfaces.

Sheet-metal screws are available in slotted, Phillips, hex and Robertson head design. Robertson, or square-drive, screws require a special screwdriver. Square-drive screws lend themselves well to using cordless electric drills for taking the drudgery out of screwing work to plates. The only problem with the electric drill is that it's easy to over-tighten and strip the thread.

I prefer to use hex-head sheet-metal screws and a "speeder," which is a cranklike automotive tool for turning bolts quickly. A speeder takes ⅜-in. sockets directly and works much like a bit brace. It allows quick, positive and painless turning of the screws without the risk of stripping them. Another advantage of hex-head screws is that they can be easily

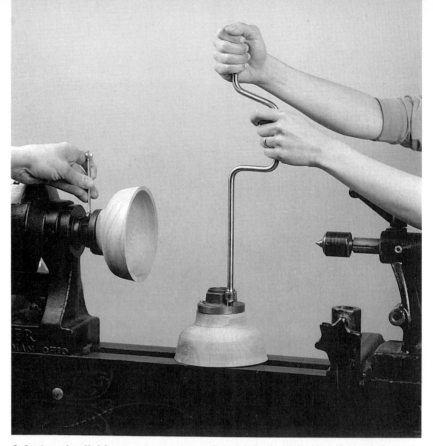

A fast and reliable way to secure a faceplate to the workpiece is to use hex-head sheet-metal screws and a speeder (right). If the screws come loose once the work is mounted on the lathe, they can be tightened with a box wrench (left).

tightened with a small box wrench once the faceplate is mounted on the headstock spindle. It's not unusual for one or more of the faceplate screws to come loose while the lathe is running, and with other screw designs you have to unscrew the faceplate from the spindle to tighten them.

Special-purpose commercial chucks

Centers and faceplates are the two basic ways of holding work on the lathe. They'll cope with the majority of your turning requirements; indeed you could turn for a lifetime using nothing more. There are times, however, when other chucking methods can make life easier. Special-purpose chucks can be invaluable for grabbing odd-shaped work, small work and finished work that requires modification. In production work, a special-purpose chuck can often speed things up considerably. In the remainder of this chapter we'll look at the vast ar-

ray of special-purpose chucks that you can buy or make yourself. With
this information, you'll be able to tackle any turning job with safety
and confidence.

Three- and four-jaw scroll chucks

Scroll chucks are crossovers from metalworking. A steel body encases
three or four jaws that open or close in unison by the action of a circular scroll plate. The jaws grip around the end of the workpiece. In metalworking chucks, the scroll plate is usually actuated by means of a key
acting through bevel gears. To save expense, woodturning scroll
chucks are usually made without the bevel gears and instead use steel
levers that fit into holes in the two halves of the chuck body to allow
turning the scroll plate directly. The Nova and small Oneway chucks
(shown above) operate this way. The large Oneway chuck uses a novel
approach—a key fits in a hole in the chuck body and in effect becomes
a bevel gear.

For woodturning, a four-jaw scroll chuck is much more satisfactory
than the three-jaw variety because four jaws will grip squares nicely.
Although you may be tempted to use a surplus metalturning chuck, it
doesn't work as well. Even if the metalworking chuck is of the four-
jaw variety, the jaws are not designed for holding wood. They're too
small and tend to indent wood without ever centering it. The jaws are
real knuckle-busters, too.

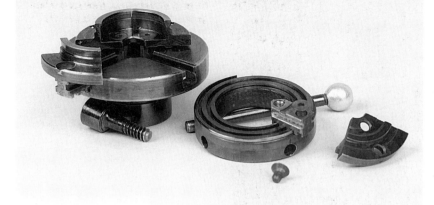

The Nova chuck (shown here disassembled) grips the workpiece with four jaws, which can be adjusted with a scroll (at right). The Nova has a variety of interchangeable jaws.

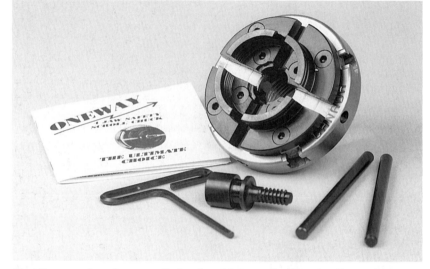

The Oneway four-jaw scroll chuck, which works like the Nova chuck, comes with a screw-chuck accessory (shown at center) and a variety of other accessories.

Scroll chucks made specifically for woodturning have jaws that hold over a much greater surface area. On most, the top half of the jaws can be unscrewed. In this way, two or more sets of jaws can be supplied, each with a different diameter grip range. On some scroll chucks, four plates with numerous tapped holes in their face can be mounted in place of the jaws. By screwing rubber posts to the plates at strategic positions, odd shapes can be held. An example would be holding a nearly finished bowl by the rim so that the base could be turned.

Scroll chucks are quick and easy to use and leave no screw holes and few other visible marks on the workpiece. They're ideal for holding small furniture parts such as knobs and finials. A handy way to work with a scroll chuck is to feed standard-sized dowel through the head-

stock spindle then through the chuck itself. (The advantage of using dowel for turning is that it doesn't have to be trued round first.) As each small piece is finished and cut off, the dowel can be advanced through the chuck ready for turning the next piece.

We tend to think of scroll chucks gripping by compressing around the outside of the work, but they can also be expanded inside a recess in the work (which could be a pedestal, a bowl or a small tabletop). Woodturning scroll chucks are angled on the outside faces of the jaws. If a dovetailed (undercut) recess is scraped in the work, as shown above, the chuck can be expanded to hold securely. This is one of the scroll chuck's most useful features.

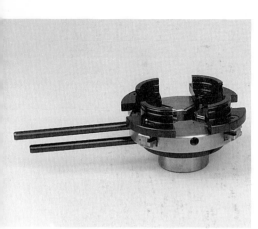

A safety feature on the Oneway chuck prevents the jaws from extending more than halfway.

Safety concerns with scroll chucks are twofold. First, the spinning jaws present an ever-present danger. At best, they're real knuckle-busters; at worst, they can maim. Second, inadvertently extending a jaw beyond the grip of the scroll will cause one or more jaws to go ballistic when you start the lathe. To ensure a firm grip by the scroll, never extend the jaw more than halfway out of the chuck body. I once overextended the jaws of a scroll chuck when using a metal lathe. A 9-lb. jaw ricocheted off the lathe carriage, went through a Thermopane window and landed 10 ft. from the building. I've never disobeyed the halfway rule since.

The Oneway chuck (shown at left) has a safety feature that prevents the jaws from extending more than halfway. This feature, combined with its excellent manufacture, makes the Oneway a particularly useful scroll chuck.

Collet chucks

Collet chucks are also crossovers from metalturning. At its simplest, a collet is a metal tube that's partially slotted lengthwise. A taper on the outside of the tube engages a threaded bezel, which holds the collet in the body of the chuck. Tightening the bezel compresses the collet, which in turn grips the work. The range of sizes that a collet chuck can grip (the "grip range") is limited to the distance between the slots running down the sides—$\frac{1}{16}$ in. on most collets. Most collet chucks come with two to three collets of standard sizes—$\frac{1}{2}$ in., $\frac{3}{4}$ in., 1 in., etc.

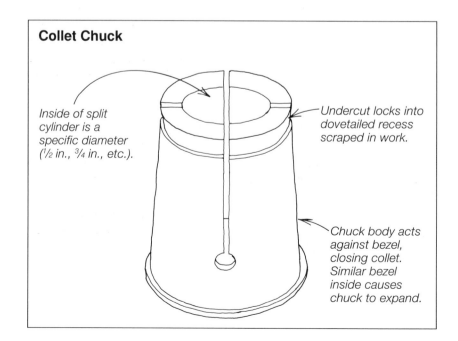

Collet Chuck

Inside of split cylinder is a specific diameter ($\frac{1}{2}$ in., $\frac{3}{4}$ in., etc.).

Undercut locks into dovetailed recess scraped in work.

Chuck body acts against bezel, closing collet. Similar bezel inside causes chuck to expand.

The Multistar chuck, shown here with interchangeable collets, wrenches, and screw-chuck and pin-chuck accessories, is a top-quality collet chuck.

Collet chucks are not used as much as scroll chucks in woodturning today. They tend to be more expensive because they require a high level of manufacture to be effective, and their narrow grip range limits their usefulness. However, collet chucks are useful for turning small pieces, especially from standard-size dowel. To mount work in a collet chuck, a tenon of the appropriate collet diameter is turned on the end of the work. (In England, a tenon is called a spigot, so a collet chuck is known as a spigot chuck.) As with scroll chucks, some collets are undercut on their end, which allows them to be expanded into a dovetailed recess in the work. Many collet chucks, such as the Multistar chuck shown above, come with a vast array of accessories that turn them into other types of chucks, such as screw chucks and pin chucks.

Screw chucks

A screw chuck is an old favorite among woodturners for holding small items, though it can also hold work as large as a dinner plate. The traditional design is simplicity itself. A wood screw protrudes from the face of the chuck. A small hole, the body diameter of the screw, is drilled in the work to facilitate threading it onto the chuck. Since a right-hand thread opposes the rotation direction of the lathe, the work self-tightens on the chuck. Work can be chucked and unchucked from a screw chuck with fair consistency.

Screw chucks are ideal for holding small work. Shown here from left to right are the Oneway scroll chuck with screw-chuck accessory, a shopmade screw chuck, and two screw chucks built on Morse-taper blanks.

Traditionally, screw chucks were small and built on a Morse-taper blank. These screw chucks are perfect for turning repetitive parts such as chess pieces and drawer pulls. The small screw leaves little visible evidence of turning (and the screw hole is usually concealed on the finished piece anyway).

A second type of screw chuck is built on a faceplate-like body or mounts in a collet or scroll chuck, which allows it to be threaded onto the headstock spindle. The more positive drive of the threaded mount makes it possible to use a much larger screw. Such chucks have a screw with a straight body and a very coarse 45° thread profile. The thread looks much like that on a drywall screw and makes for a very positive hold in wood. This type of screw chuck is good for larger items such as furniture bases, trays, plates and even small bowls.

Pin chucks

A pin chuck is a favorite of bowl turners. It allows safe and positive mounting of irregularly shaped chunks of wood. The pin chuck's one drawback is that it requires drilling a fairly deep hole into the work. This hole matches the pin and is usually 1 in. in diameter. The deep hole does not present a problem in bowl turning because it can be drilled into the mouth of the bowl, and this area will be scooped out anyway. (You use the pin chuck just to work on the base and outside of the bowl, then mount the bowl on another chuck to work on the inside.)

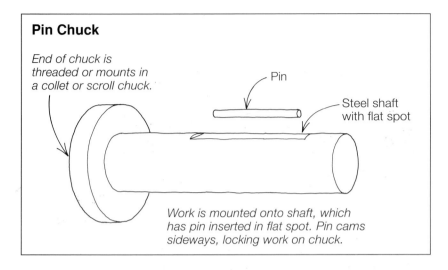

Pin Chuck

End of chuck is threaded or mounts in a collet or scroll chuck.

Pin

Steel shaft with flat spot

Work is mounted onto shaft, which has pin inserted in flat spot. Pin cams sideways, locking work on chuck.

There is a flat spot milled on the body of the chuck. Before inserting the body into the drilled hole, a small metal pin is placed in the milled flat spot. Once the work is fully onto the chuck, turning it will cause the pin to cam sideways, locking everything tight. The chuck can be home-fabricated by welding a length of 1-in. cold rolled steel to a nut or an old faceplate. The flat spot can be filed and a nail used for the pin.

Jacobs chuck

Correctly called a "drill chuck," the Jacobs chuck is an old stalwart that is more often named for its original American manufacturer. The head of the chuck has an outer ring and an inner ring that encloses the jaws. Turning the outer ring with a key causes the jaws to open and close. The drill chuck mounts into the lathe on a Morse-taper shaft, which is a separate piece that fits into the back of the chuck on a short Jarno taper. Morse-taper "backs" can be purchased in any combination of Morse and Jarno tapers. If you have a drill chuck that does not fit your lathe, you can buy replacement backs from any machine-tool supplier. Also, smaller tapers can be adapted to larger spindle sockets with taper-sleeve adapters (see the photo on p. 11).

The main use for drill chucks is to hold drill bits in either the head-stock or the tailstock, but they can also be used to grip small work such as knobs and miniature turnings. Drill chucks are sold according to the largest diameter they can grip. Common sizes are $\frac{3}{8}$ in. and $\frac{1}{2}$ in., with the latter being better for woodturning lathes. Delta used to offer a very large Jacobs chuck, called a headstock chuck, which was threaded in the back and screwed onto their 1 in. x 8 TPI spindle. I have one and use it frequently. Although this type of chuck is no longer available, I see them from time to time at flea markets and used machinery dealers.

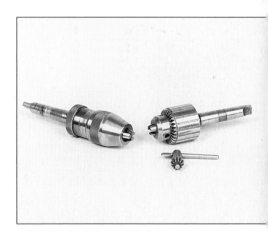

Drill chucks (also called Jacobs chucks) are used primarily for drilling in the lathe, but they can also hold small work effectively.

Shopmade and improvised chucks

I firmly believe that the best chuck is one you make yourself. Most shopmade chucks can be fabricated from scrap wood, so they cost next to nothing. I think this is one of the major reasons they're not used more often—as woodworkers, we tend to distrust any chuck we didn't pay big bucks for. That a free chuck could work better than an expensive model is mind-boggling.

Economy aside, shopmade chucks have several other advantages over special-purpose store-bought chucks. First, they'll usually hold better and more securely. Second, unlike their commercial cousins that tend to mar the work, shopmade chucks leave little or no trace of their presence. Third, they allow you to turn balls and other objects that just couldn't be turned in a metal chuck. Finally, your design is free with improvised chucks—you make the chuck fit your design, so the design comes first, which is the way it should be. Too often with manufactured chucks we knowingly or subconsciously make the work fit the chuck.

Shopmade chucks have a lot in common with jigs and fixtures—you always put off making them, but once you do make them you wonder how you got along without them! Chucks are actually very easy to build, requiring only basic woodworking skills and rarely more than 15 minutes of your time. Here, we'll look at the various types, including jam chucks, tapered mandrels, paper joints, double-sided tape, glue blocks, screw chucks and pressure turning. I must warn you, however, that improvised chucks are a way of thinking rather than a prescribed dogma. As long as a chuck holds the work securely, there's no right or wrong way of making it. I hope that the following will get your creative juices flowing, so you can start to devise your own methods of chucking to suit the work you want to turn. Don't be afraid to experiment.

Jam chucks

One of the simplest and oldest homemade chucks is the jam, or cup, chuck. It's a sure, simple way to grab small items without leaving marks in the work. I use it to hold anything from knobs and finials to trays and small bowls.

The body of a jam chuck should be spindle-turned from a 3-in. to 4-in. diameter piece of close-grained hardwood. Maple, ash or beech all work very well. Since scrap stock this diameter is hard to come by, I usually glue two pieces of 8/4 stock together. Yellow glue works fine, but be sure to plane both surfaces for a perfect joint, use plenty of glue

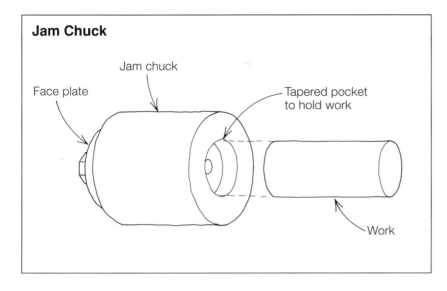

Jam Chuck

Face plate

Jam chuck

Tapered pocket
to hold work

Work

and clamp for a full 24 hours. In the old days a tap hole was drilled through the center of the billet and it was threaded to screw directly onto the headstock spindle (see the bottom photo on p. 54). Since suitable wood taps are unavailable today and wood threads do not work out well in end grain anyway, it's easier to screw the billet to a faceplate. (Remember I suggested to buy extra faceplates?) Attach a 3-in. to 5-in. section of the billet to the faceplate with 1-in. or 1½-in. sheet-metal screws (as explained above in the faceplate section).

As shown in the photos on pp. 52-53, mount the faceplate in your lathe and true up the outside diameter of the billet with a spindle gouge. Face the end, and drill a ⅜-in. hole through the center with a drill bit mounted in the tailstock (for more about drilling in the lathe, see pp. 136-139). The drill hole allows you to use a knockout bar to eject the work.

Next, scrape a tapered pocket into the face of the chuck that is the diameter of the work you want to hold. The taper should be about 3° inclusive (the same angle as a Morse taper). To cut the taper, I use a special scraper that can easily be ground from an old file and a long-forgotten auxiliary tool rest, called an arm rest (for more about scrapers and the arm rest, see p. 97). You'll quickly find the right taper—if it's too steep or not steep enough, the chuck won't hold the work.

Making and Using a Jam Chuck

1. Attach a faceplate to the end of the chuck blank.

2. True up the body of the chuck and square the end face.

3. Drill a hole through the center of the chuck.

4. Scrape a tapered pocket the diameter of the work to be held into the end face of the chuck.

5. Fit the work (shown here is a blank for a lidded box) into the pocket.

6. Tap the work into the pocket, and true up as necessary.

7. You're now free to work on the piece. Here, a spindle gouge is used to turn the outside of the box.

Jam chucks are used primarily to hold small items in the lathe, but bowls can also be jam-chucked to allow turning of the base and outside.

Most work for jam chucking is turned between centers or on a faceplate before it's mounted in the jam chuck. Remember to turn the edge of the work face that will go into the jam chuck square. Insert the work into the chuck by lining it up as square as possible and giving it a solid rap with your hammer. Now turn the lathe over by hand, watching for eccentricity. Rap the edge opposite the point that is most eccentric and retest. Continue until the work is perfectly centered. Rubbing some blackboard chalk on the walls of the pocket will add greatly to the chuck's holding power.

To use a jam chuck you have to be able to turn well enough that a catch is the exception rather than the rule, since a catch can throw the work from the lathe. Jam-chucking is a skill, so the first few times will be an uphill battle; once learned it will become second nature. Just remember Conover's First Law of Jam-Chucking: "Thou shalt not jam-chuck anything thou art not prepared to be hit in the head with." Jam-chucking is best used for small items, such as the box shown in the photo story on pp. 52-53. Having said this, I've successfully chucked items as big as boccie balls. I jam-chuck bowls regularly, but this is with the added security of trapping the work in the chuck with a tailstock.

Up until the early part of this century a turner would typically have a range of jam chucks made from gun metal by a local machinist. They worked splendidly. I've seen a 20th-century version of the jam chuck in which it's turned into a collet chuck. The outside of the chuck is gently turned, and the cup is partially split by bandsawing or backsawing (shown below). A wood or metal ring is then pounded onto the taper to force the collet closed. (Don't be tempted to use automotive hose clamps—they don't have the closing power for this task.)

Antique smoking-pipe chucks are a cross between jam chucks and collet chucks. A wood ring is slipped over the chuck to force the collet closed around the work.

Tapered mandrels

Tapered mandrels are essentially jam chucks turned inside out. They're a good way to hold small items such as napkin rings, and a great way to hold hollow spindle turnings between centers. The advantages of tapered mandrels are that the outside of the work can be turned concentric with the bore and that the work can be chucked and unchucked quickly and held safely.

To mount an item such as a napkin ring, start with a turned billet of wood on a faceplate, just as when making a jam chuck. However, to make a tapered mandrel, turn the outside to a gentle 3° taper. The partially turned napkin ring is placed over the mandrel and, using a block of wood and a hammer, alternately "adjusted" until it runs true. The outer surfaces of the napkin ring can now be finish-turned and sanded.

Depending on the size of the central hole, hollow spindle turnings can be mounted on the lathe with tapered plugs or tapered end caps. Tapered plugs are used for cylindrical objects (such as a pepper mill) with a fairly small central bore—anything up to about 1 in. inside diameter (see the top drawing on p. 56). Turn the plugs as a single piece between centers and then saw them apart. Tap the plugs into the ends of the turning and remount on the lathe on the original center marks. The outside of the object can now be turned concentric with the bore.

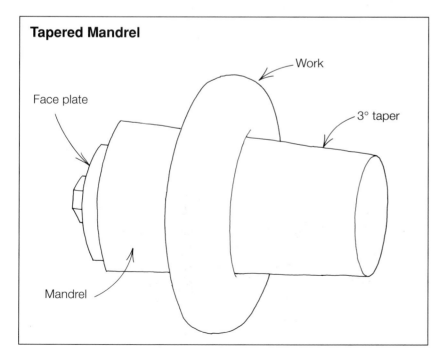

Tapered Mandrel

Work

Face plate

3° taper

Mandrel

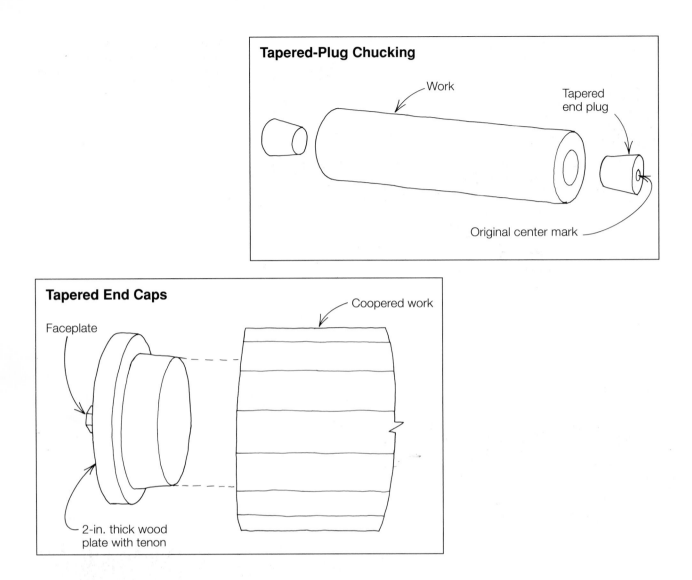

Tapered-Plug Chucking

Work

Tapered
end plug

Original center mark

Tapered End Caps

Faceplate

Coopered work

2-in. thick wood
plate with tenon

Tapered end caps are used with hollow work that has a large central bore. This is often coopered work (glued up out of staves), such as bird houses, buckets and columns. An important difference from tapered plugs is that the mandrel for each end is faceplate-turned as a separate item. A good way to hold each end cap is to use a large screw chuck, which allows the tapered step in the mandrel to be turned concentric with a center hole. As in the case of the coopered bird house shown in the top photos on the facing page, the headstock mandrel can be left on the screw chuck. The tailstock mandrel is inserted into the work and the center hole left by the screw chuck is caught by a 60° live center. The work is now safely trapped between centers on the set of mandrels and can be turned easily. I've chucked 12-in. diameter by 8-ft. long coopered columns using this method.

The second consideration is that sufficient pressure must be applied to the tape joint to achieve adequate adhesion. The joint should either be clamped or pressed in a vise for a few seconds (advancing the tailstock spindle can also provide sufficient pressure). Many turners tape the work directly to a faceplate, which works fine with standard Delta-style flat-faced plates. My preference for faceplates with a raised lip at the edge renders them unsuitable for tape, though this can be overcome by screwing a block of wood to the faceplate and then scraping it flat (see the instructions for flattening a glue block below).

Other than using fabric-based tape and applying sufficient pressure to hold the joint, the principles of chucking with double-sided tape are the same as those for the paper joint.

Glue blocks

For faceplate work such as a stool top, the work is often simply screwed directly to the faceplate. Since the screw holes are on the bottom of the stool, they will be seen only by the snoopy. The trend today among professional woodturners is to leave no trace of chucking. One way to avoid screw holes in the work when using a faceplate is to leave extra stock at the base of the piece and then cut above the screws. A less wasteful way to avoid screw holes is to use a glue block.

To make a glue block, bandsaw a hardwood block of sufficient thickness to bury the screws to a diameter slightly larger than the faceplate. This block is then glued to the center of the work. It is imperative to use a good-quality glue and achieve a joinery-level fit between the work and glue block. Often, the easiest course is to run one side of the work though a jointer before it is bandsawn into rounds. Alternatively, each round can be hand-planed after sawing. Hand-planing is the option I prefer because it leaves an underside free of planer marks and gives the best of all possible glue joints.

The glue block itself should be jointed and thickness-planed before it is bandsawn round. Even then the face of the glue block may not be square to the axis of the lathe—either because the planer is a bit out of square or the faceplate is not true. The best course is to mount the glue block to the faceplate and scrape it square with a large dome scraper. When the face is dead flat with a straightedge, it is square to the headstock spindle.

However you achieve the joinery-level fit between the block and the work, use plenty of glue and clamp the joint for 24 hours before turning. Once the work is mounted, test the joint with a good two-handed tug. After you've finished turning the work, remove the glue block by paring most of it away with a sharp bench chisel and mallet, then hand-plane the glue line away.

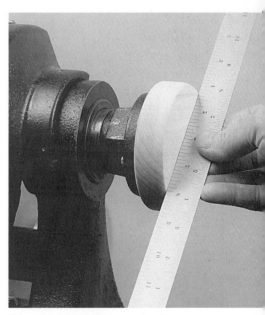

Use a straightedge to check a glue block for flatness.

Screw chucks

Traditionally, screw chucks were made at the lathe by the turner, but now, as we've seen, manufactured screw chucks are readily available. However, I still think that home-made screw chucks are superior to commercial models for holding items such as knobs, finials and chess pieces. One great advantage is that the face of the chuck can be turned to the base diameter of the workpiece, which makes duplication of additional pieces an easy task. Additionally, the screw in the chuck can be matched to the screw that will install the finished turning.

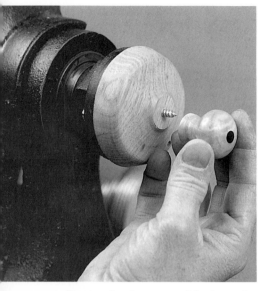

Screw chucks are an ideal way to hold small work in the lathe.

To make a screw chuck, start with a 1-in. to 1¼-in. thick glue block. Scrape the face of the glue block to the base diameter of the workpiece (shown in the photo at left). Then drill a small hole for the screw in the center of the block with a drill bit secured in a chuck in the tailstock. Remove the faceplate from the headstock, and screw a suitable wood or sheet-metal screw into the hole in the back of the glue block. Applying some epoxy or cyanoacrylate ("super") glue to the screw thread will prevent it from unscrewing during mounting of work. The screw should protrude about ⅜ in. from the face of the block.

Pressure turning

A pressure hold is a dandy way to chuck lightweight, flat, round items such as plates. This improvised chuck may also be used to hold work while scraping a dovetail recess for expanding scroll and collet chucks (see the photo and discussion on pp. 45-46).

To prepare for pressure turning, file the nail protruding from the glue block to a point.

The basis of a pressure-holding chuck is a glue block scraped flat, as described above. Using a drill chuck in the tailstock, drill a pilot hole slightly smaller than a 10d nail at the center of the glue block but only three-quarters of the way through. Pound a 10d nail into the hole so that it bottoms out. Cut off the nail about ¹⁄₁₆ in. proud of the face of the block and file it to a point. The pointing operation is easily accomplished by touching a file to the nail with the lathe running.

Since rounds are laid out with a compass, there will be a center mark on the workpiece. Align this mark on the nail point and force the work against the glue block with the tailstock spindle. You can either do this with a flat live center point in the tailstock or interpose a small block of wood between a cup center or 60° point and the work. Gluing 180-grit sandpaper to the face of the glue block will provide more positive drive to the work.

Using a pressure-holding chuck, flat work can be completely turned on both sides, except for a small nub under the center point. This nub can be chiseled away and sanded smooth once the piece is removed from the lathe. The only sign of chucking will be a small indent at the center of the plate base.

Mount work for pressure turning between the nail block and a flat center in the tailstock.

Both sides of the work can be turned in their entirety, except for the small nub under the tailstock center.

CHAPTER 3
Turning Tools

Lathes are unlike saws, jointers and other woodworking machines in that the machine itself doesn't do the cutting. Instead, the operator holds a tool against the rotating workpiece and cuts away the unnecessary wood to obtain the desired shape. Different operations require different tools, and in this chapter I'll explore the various tools that are needed for spindle turning and faceplate turning, as well as those that can be used for either operation.

Using the right tool for the right job is only half the battle—the key to successful turning is a sharp tool. I've observed that most beginners are quick to blame themselves for lack of skill when something goes wrong. Invariably their problems can be traced to tools that are dull or ground to incorrect angles. When I place a correctly sharpened tool in their hands, they're amazed to find that they had the skill to turn all along.

Sharpening employs the same skills necessary for turning, but while most neophytes are eager to master the intricacies of turning, many are intimidated by sharpening. Since sharp tools are necessary to be able to turn at all, sharpening is a skill that must be mastered. Rest assured, if you have the skill to turn (and you do), you have the skill to sharpen. To understand sharpening, you must first understand how tools cut. I know, you're anxious to learn how to *use* your turning tools, but be patient, we'll get there in due course.

Sharp tools are the key to successful turning. Here, a spindle gouge is ground to a 30° bevel.

Cutting theory

To cut properly, tools require the correct rake, clearance and grind angles. The rake angle is the inclusive angle from the top surface, or back, of the tool to the surface of the work (see the drawing below). The clearance is the angular space between the bevel of the tool and the surface of the work. The grind angle is the inclusive angle from the back of the tool to the bevel. While tools such as hand planes and planer blades require clearance to work, turning tools generally cut with 0° clearance. This is because turning tools cut with the bevel rubbing against the work. Thus the rake angle of a properly working turning tool is the same as the grind angle.

At its simplest, a turning tool is a rectangular piece of metal whose end is ground to a 30° angle. This 30° grind creates the bevel, which starts at the cutting edge and ends at the heel (see the drawing at top, facing page). To understand how a turning tool cuts, it's simplest first to use the example of cutting into a flat board rather than a cylindrical work-piece. The tool can cut in one of three ways, as shown in the drawing

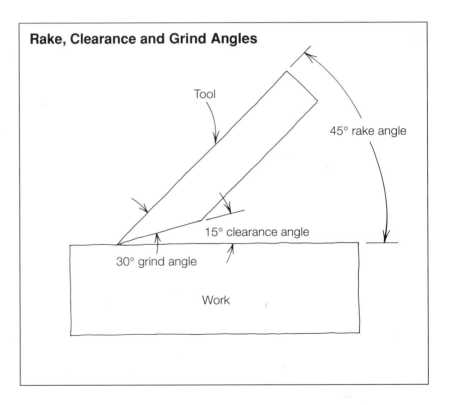

Rake, Clearance and Grind Angles

Tool

45° rake angle

15° clearance angle

30° grind angle

Work

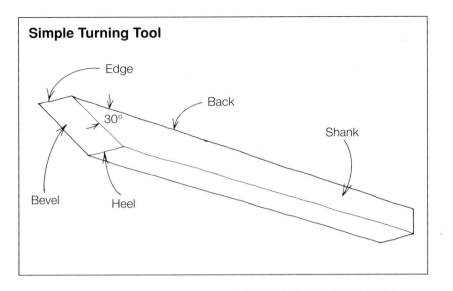

Simple Turning Tool

Edge

Back

30°

Shank

Bevel

Heel

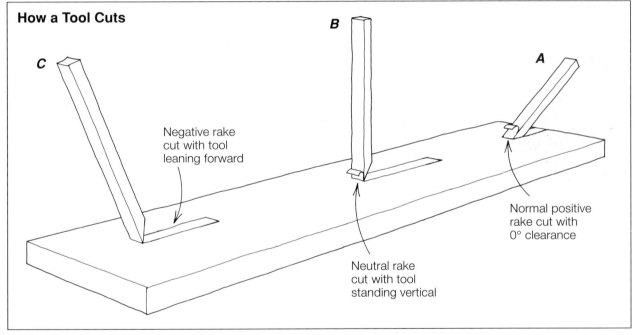

How a Tool Cuts

C

B

A

Negative rake
cut with tool
leaning forward

Normal positive
rake cut with
0° clearance

Neutral rake
cut with tool
standing vertical

above. We would normally cut into the surface of a board with the
chisel as in drawing A. An optimum cut is obtained by placing the tool
on the bevel and rocking forward until the tool just cuts—this is the
shear cut we should strive for when turning. We control the depth of
the cut by rocking up and down on the bevel, which essentially acts as
a fulcrum.

As we raise the tool up off the bevel we'll still raise a chip until somewhere around vertical, which would bring us to a neutral rake angle, as shown in drawing B on p. 65. The problem is, however, that as we raise the tool upward we can no longer control the depth of cut because the bevel is no longer acting as a fulcrum, and the tool will tend to dig in. This is the scrape cut we should try to avoid when turning.

If we keep leaning the tool forward past vertical it moves into negative rake and stops raising a chip altogether. Material will still be removed if sufficient downward force is exerted on the tool, but we'll now be making a plow cut, which leaves a poor finish and generates considerable heat. Plow cutting is inefficient and is not used in woodworking; it should not be confused with the seemingly negative rake-angle cut made with a burred-edge scraper (see pp. 96-97).

The lower the angle of attack by the tool, the less effort required to push it, but the more wedgelike it becomes. As the tool becomes more wedgelike, the tendency to split the wood ahead of the cutting edge increases. Although you might think that the angle of grind (30°) would limit the minimum angle of attack, this is not necessarily the case. The rake angle will be 30° only when the tool is square to the direction of travel. By skewing the cutting edge to the direction of travel, an even lower attack angle can be obtained. With the edge skewed 45° to the direction of travel, the effective rake angle becomes less than 20°, as shown in the drawing below. A good way to visualize this concept is to compare walking straight up a hill with walking up at an

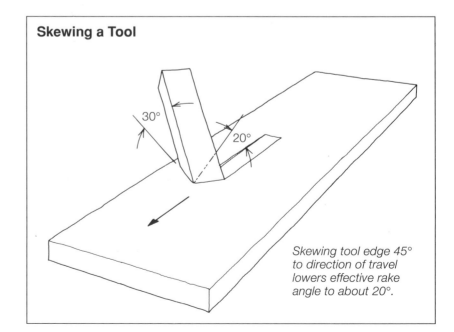

Skewing a Tool

30°

20°

Skewing tool edge 45° to direction of travel lowers effective rake angle to about 20°.

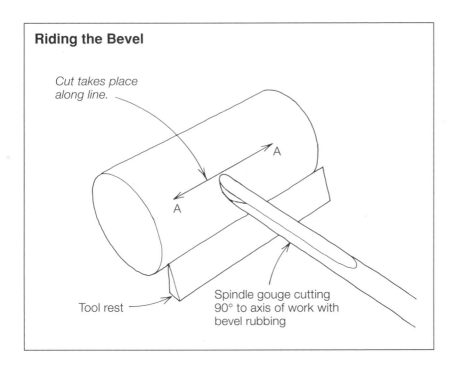

Riding the Bevel

Cut takes place along line.

A

A

Tool rest

Spindle gouge cutting 90° to axis of work with bevel rubbing

angle. Although the latter is a longer distance, the grade is much more gentle. As you turn, there will be many instances where you will cut with the tool at an angle, but if tearout is a problem you should return the tool to 90°.

The ideal presentation of a woodturning tool is shown in the drawing above. This is essentially the same case as in drawing A on p. 65, except that the flat board is now a circular workpiece and the tool has the additional support of the tool rest. The tool is also more likely to be one of several compound shapes (a spindle gouge is shown in the drawing). We want to ride the bevel with the edge cutting along the line AA. To achieve this, the heel of the bevel is pressed against the work first, then the tool is slid backwards and down on the rest until it just starts to cut. Raising or lowering the tool rest will raise or lower line AA.

These are the rudiments of how we want a turning tool to cut. We'll become much more intimate with the details of how and why as we progress, but for now this simple model will suffice. All of our cutting theory has assumed that the tool is sharp, so let's now digress for a moment and explore just what defines a sharp edge and how to make an edge sharp if it is not.

Sharpening

A sharp edge is formed when two planes come together at an angle. The meeting point of the two planes allows us to concentrate force at an edge and so cut wood. For woodturning tools, the included angle between the two planes is more often than not 30°. The bevel or bevels leading up to the edge need to be a perfectly flat plane or a slight hollow grind of constant radius (the hollow grind results when the tool is held against the round edge of the grinding wheel).

The two steps in the sharpening process are grinding the cutting edge to the desired shape and angle and then honing the edge to create a razor-sharp edge. Faceplate tools and scrapers can usually be used straight from the grinder. Spindle-turning tools, however, require a high-quality surface finish at the cutting edge so the tool is free of feather. A feather, or wire edge, is the tendency of the steel to form a thin ribbon of foil at the cutting edge. Often called a burr, this foil rolls over the edge, effectively turning it into a radius rather than two planes meeting perfectly. Bringing the edge to a polish (or a near polish) eliminates this feather edge.

Grinding

Thus far, I've talked a lot about cutting theory and tool geometry; now it's time to look at the actual mechanics of how you translate this theory into practice. That brings us to grinding, the starting point in the sharpening process. You'll have to grind new tools that you buy, since they rarely come from the factory ground to the correct angle, let alone sharp. You'll also have to regrind your tools as they wear in use. In these endeavors, the bench grinder will be your constant companion.

Grinders   Bench grinders for home use up through light-industrial use come in 6-in., 7-in. and 10-in. sizes (grinder size is specified according to the diameter of the grinding wheels). The smaller two sizes are generally built on a 3,300-rpm motor frame, while the larger is on a 1,725-rpm frame. Although many think the larger machine grinds cooler because of the slower speed, there's really no significant difference (5,182 feet per minute for the 6-in. grinder vs. 4,516 feet per minute for the 10-in. grinder). There is, however, a gain in control at slower speeds.

Much more important than the speed of the grinder are other features, such as the rests, safety shields, lighting, guards, wheels and means of dressing the wheels. The rest, in particular, is a most important detail. All grinders are equipped with a rest to support the tool during grinding, but most rests are woefully inadequate for sharpening woodturning tools. Economy grinders usually have a fixed, one-piece cast-iron or aluminum rest that allows grinding only at 90°, which is fine for the

needs of metalworkers but of little use to woodturners, since most turning tools are ground to 30°. Better grinders have an articulated rest that can be adjusted at any angle to the grinding wheel, which is a great help in presenting the tool at the correct angle for grinding.

If you have a grinder with a fixed rest, you can modify the rest so it can be used with turning tools. To do this, attach a wood wedge to the top of the rest with double-sided tape or sheet-metal screws. Some finagling is necessary to get the right angle, and the angle changes as the wheel wears. A better solution is to make or buy an auxiliary rest to replace the original. You can make an adjustable rest quite easily from some scrap plywood, a carriage bolt, a washer and a wing nut.

I recently bought a Oneway auxiliary rest (see Sources of Supply on pp. 191-192) for my grinder (shown in the photo on p. 70), and I've been very pleased with the results. The rest mounts to the table or bench in front of the grinder, replacing the original. Since my grinder is on a pedestal, I had to mount a sheet of plywood between the pedestal and the grinder to accommodate the Oneway system. The Oneway comes with a variety of rests and accessories well suited to the needs of a woodturner. In addition to a large, highly adjustable platform rest, it has a simple bar-type rest (made from ½-in. bar stock) that's perfect for sharpening woodturning tools, especially gouges.

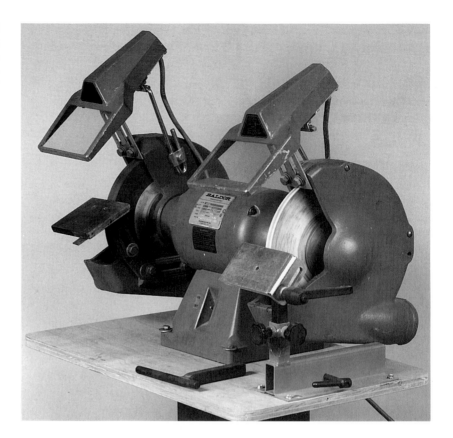

Adding an articulated replacement rest to the grinder makes it possible to grind turning tools at any angle. Note also the metal-framed safety shields on this grinder.

In his book *Practical Woodturner* (Sterling, 1990), Frank Pain recommends mounting a grinding wheel in the lathe and using the lathe tool rest to support the tool during grinding. His logic is that this arrangement emulates the process of actual turning and is more natural to a turner. He's right, but the problem is that an unguarded grinding wheel spinning in your lathe is unsafe. The Oneway bar rest gives you a lathe-type tool rest on any grinder. You have the safety of the enclosed wheel with the convenience of a lathe-type rest. Additionally, the Oneway has a handy diamond dresser (see p. 72) that ensures that the wheel is both perfectly round and flat side to side.

Traditionally, the safety shields on any grinder were metal frames with tempered safety glass in them. Sadly, most grinders today are supplied with plastic viewing shields without metal frames (as shown in the photo on p. 69). The problem with plastic shields is that hot metal sparks burn right into them, and the plastic gathers dust by static attraction. If your grinder has plastic shields in a metal frame, I recommend replacing them with safety-glass shields, which you will have to have custom made (for a cost of about $75). The shields should have two layers of tempered safety glass with a sheet of plastic sandwiched in between, which makes shattering near impossible. If you must make do with plastic shields, some antistatic spray from a computer shop helps prevent dust buildup on the surface.

The safety shields provide a good degree of protection against flying sparks, but it's important that you always wear safety glasses at the grinder. If your glasses don't have side shields, then goggles or a face shield are in order.

Good lighting at a grinder is a must. Although industrial grinders often have lighting built into the safety-shield frames, manufacturers of economy grinders typically leave lighting to the end user. A simple gooseneck lamp will suffice to provide direct local lighting.

Any grinder should provide guarding that encloses the wheel except at the area just above the rest. An open, unguarded wheel should not be used under any circumstances. Most grinders have a sliding shield, or "spark arrester," at the top edge of the guard. In addition to containing sparks inside the guard, this shield helps to contain shrapnel should the wheel explode. It should be adjusted to within $\frac{1}{16}$ in. of the wheel surface, and as the wheel is dressed (see p. 72) it should be readjusted. The rest should also be kept within $\frac{1}{8}$ in. of the wheel surface at all times.

A good practice with a new wheel, whether it's a replacement or one that came with a new grinder, is to stand to one side, start the machine then leave the room for a few minutes. If there is a defect in the wheel it will usually disintegrate at, or shortly after, startup. Never start the grinder without all guards securely in place.

Most grinders are delivered with silicon-carbide wheels. These wheels can be used for grinding almost anything from steel to glass and bathroom tiles, but they tend to grind hot for steel. A better choice for tool grinding is an aluminum-oxide wheel, which is sometimes called a "pink wheel" (though it's often blue or white). The bonding material for aluminum-oxide wheels is much softer than for silicon-carbide, so these wheels are of little use for grinding materials other than steel. Aluminum-oxide wheels are available at industrial tool suppliers.

A common mistake among beginners is to grind with too fine a wheel. A good roughing wheel is 60 to 80 grit, while the finishing wheel should be 100 to 120 grit. For bench grinding you should never use a wheel finer than 150 grit. Bear in mind that the grit of powered abrasives is never as coarse as hand sandpaper, which is what we generally judge abrasive grit by, because each particle of abrasive penetrates less when moving at speed.

A diamond dresser is used to true a new grinding wheel and to sharpen the wheel's surface when it gets clogged with metal.

A new wheel, whether it came with the grinder or is a replacement, is never perfectly round. It's impossible to grind well on such a wheel because the tool will just hop up and down. Thus, it's essential to have some means of truing your grinding wheel. This truing operation is referred to as "dressing." The best way to dress the wheel is to use a diamond dresser, which is simply an industrial diamond brazed into the end of a piece of cold-rolled steel. By setting the shank on the grinding rest and sliding the diamond tip laterally across the grinding wheel, the wheel will be kissed off round. The diamond dresser should be presented at right angles to the face of the wheel in a scrape cut and with a fairly light touch.

Fortunately, industrial diamonds are cheap compared to their gem-quality cousins. A good diamond dresser will cost you between $15 and $60. Bigger dressers, called clusters, contain more than one diamond and cost about $60. Diamond dressers are available from industrial supply houses (see Sources of Supply on p. 191-192).

An alternative way to dress the grinding wheel is to use a star-wheel dresser, which is available at any hardware store. However, there are a couple of drawbacks to this kind of dresser. First, a star-wheel dresser can follow the contour of a wheel and not really make it round, which is a prime objective of the exercise. Second, I don't feel that it fractures the abrasive particles as well as a diamond dresser, and therefore produces a relatively glazed surface. There is a third type of dresser available—a silicon-carbide stick—but since it's only marginally harder than the wheel there is definite glazing, and I can't imagine why anyone would choose to use one.

A dresser is used not only to true new wheels but also to freshen the surface of wheels that have become dull. At the microscopic level, any grinding wheel (or whetstone for that matter) is nothing more than a collection of tiny cutting tools. Only about 10% of these have a positive rake and sufficient clearance to make a chip-raising cut, which explains why grinding is such an inefficient process. As you grind, the 10% of the abrasive particles that are doing the cutting become dull. The area between them fills up with metal, at which time they effectively lose their clearance. A "loaded" wheel will generate a lot of heat but have little effect on the tool. Any time you can see steel in the surface of the wheel, or when the surface looks glazed or has grooves worn in it, it's time to dress the wheel (again, preferably with a diamond dresser) to bring fresh abrasive particles to the surface.

Like driving, the actual act of grinding is more a matter of practice than anything else. When driving, a snowy parking lot is the place to learn to control skids, not a mountain road in the middle of a snow storm with an oncoming bus. So it is with grinding tools—an old file or round iron bar is a good place to start, not a brand-new $40 turning tool. Learn to set the tool on the rest, move it forward into the wheel and immediately start sliding it laterally or rolling it as dictated by the shape. Just as you must learn to feel that the bevel is flat on the work when turning, you must learn to feel that it is flat on the wheel when grinding. With practice, grinding will become second nature.

As you grind, you'll need a good-size container of cold water right next to the grinder so you can quench the tool when it gets hot. A metal tub is best; a hot tool can burn right through a plastic one. Carbon tools should never be heated much above the boiling point of water, because you start to lose the temper in some carbon-steel tools at 430°F. This is why I think high-speed-steel (HSS) turning tools are a good investment—you won't draw the temper if you overheat them during grinding (see the sidebar on p. 79).

Honing

Spindle-turning tools (and occasionally faceplate tools) require a keen edge, and this is gained through the process of honing. During honing, the finish left by the grinder is refined from a fairly rough surface finish to a polished (or near-polished) edge free of feather. After honing, your turning tool should be sharp enough to shave hair from your arm.

I use two methods to hone lathe tools—whetting with stones and buffing. I generally use both methods in any given turning session because stones work better on some tools, while buffers carry the day for others. I always use stones for the skew chisel, since a skew is the one tool that works best with an absolutely flat bevel and a keen edge. Because gouges have a compound shape, I find it easier to use a buffer on gouges of all types.

Whetstones are used with oil or water as a lubricant. The lubricant prevents metal particles from bonding into the pores of the stone. Just as with our grinding wheel, metal buildup between the abrasive particles will remove clearance and reduce the abrasive action.

Whetstones are available in a variety of types, including Arkansas oil stones, India oil stones, Japanese water stones and ceramic stones (the latter are used dry). Although some woodworkers have strong preferences about the type of stones they use, I've found that they all work about equally well. It's not so much what you use but rather understanding the process and using the correct grades of stones in the correct sequence. All types of stone come in three or more grades,

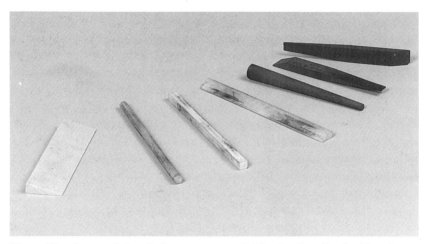

Stone files in a variety of shapes are useful for honing the inside of gouges. Shown here from left to right are an Arkansas knife-edge file, three India stones and three ceramic stones.

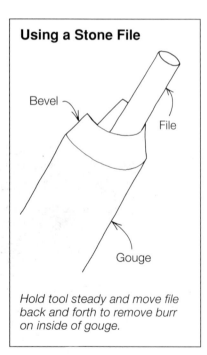

Using a Stone File

Bevel

File

Gouge

Hold tool steady and move file back and forth to remove burr on inside of gouge.

ranging from coarse to fine. Just as with sanding, the way to achieve a polish is to work up progressively through grades. India oil stones and ceramic stones are available in a variety of special shapes called stone files. They're ideal for honing complicated shapes such as the inside of gouges.

As in grinding, the knack to using flat stones to sharpen chisels is to keep the bevel absolutely flat on the stone. Place the tool down on the heel of the bevel and rock forward until you feel the bevel go flat on the stone. By locking your wrists and stroking in either a circular or a back-and-forth motion, it's possible to maintain a flat. Hold your hands as close to the bevel as you can get them. A common mistake is to place the hands too far back on the tool shank or even hold the tool by the handle. Since the heel of the bevel is a fulcrum point, the shank of the tool is a lever arm. The farther back you grip, the longer the lever arm and the less sense of feeling you have for the bevel being flat on the stone. It's a good idea to remove the tool handle if possible, because its weight can throw off your sense of feel.

Keep stroking the bevel until you feel that you have rolled a burr on the back side of the edge. At this point, turn the chisel over and whet the other bevel. The burr will be less or more pronounced depending on the grit of the stone. Now work up to the next grade of stone and keep progressing until there is no feather edge and a polish is obtained.

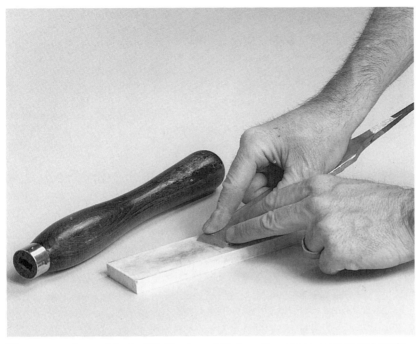

Sharpen a skew chisel with the bevel flat on the stone and your hands as close to the bevel as possible. Removing the chisel's handle gives you a better feel for the tool.

Buffing

Although many turners use only stones to hone their tools, I find that buffing is much more effective for bringing gouges to a perfect edge. Buffing is the technique of using cloth or felt wheels, spinning at high speed and charged with abrasive compound, to improve the surface finish of metal.

Many people simply mount a cloth wheel in a 6-in. bench grinder, but I don't feel that a grinder makes a good buffer because the rest and guards get in the way. In addition, grinders run too fast—at speeds much above 4,000 surface feet per minute, the wheel tends to throw compound off as fast as you can crayon it on. It's much better to make a buffer yourself. Several companies manufacture inexpensive jack shafts that are suitable for building a buffer. The shafts have a ½-in. arbor that fits readily available 6-in. diameter cloth wheels and is best powered by a ¼-hp or ⅓-hp 3,300 rpm motor. You can often find a used motor at a motor rewinder for a nominal price.

An inexpensive jack shaft mounted to a motor makes a simple buffer. (Photo courtesy of Woodcraft Supply Corp.)

Buffing wheels are used with buffing compounds to improve the surface finish of tool edges after grinding.

A buffer can be made by mounting a buffing arbor and wheel in the lathe itself.

A second way to make a small buffer for tool sharpening is to mount a buffing wheel in the lathe itself. Small arbors with a ¼-in. or ⅜-in. shank are sold for mounting a 4-in. buffing wheel in an electric drill. Mount the arbor in a drill chuck in the headstock spindle of your lathe and you have a cheap (less than $20 including the compound) and effective buffer. I first latched onto this idea out of a need to have a buffer on the road when I do seminars and demonstrations.

Buffing wheels are available in various sizes (4 in., 6 in., 8 in. and 10 in.) and two types, spiral sewn and cushion sewn, according to the way the layers of cloth that form the wheel are sewn together. As the name implies, spiral-sewn wheels are stitched in a continuous spiral from the center. They are best for use with coarser compounds when aggressive cutting action is required. Cushion-sewn wheels are stitched in concentric rings and are softer and fluffier than their spiral-sewn counterparts. These wheels are better for final polishing when gentle cutting action and a mirror finish are the goals.

Buffing compounds are usually a wax/grease and abrasive mixture. They're sold in stick form and crayoned onto the spinning wheel. Compounds are proprietary in formulation, and most are designed for use with a specific metal, though some have a more general application. Stainless-steel compound, for example, is good for final buffing of stainless steel, steel and brass.

The correct way to buff a spindle gouge is to hold the bevel at a tangent to the buffing wheel (above). Buffing at an obtuse angle (right) leaves a rounded-over bevel that's unsatisfactory.

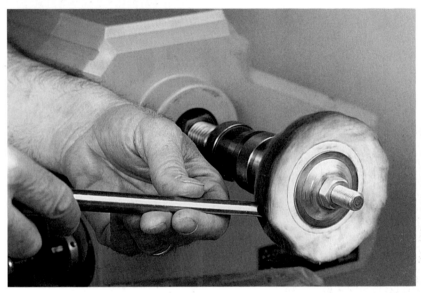

Buffing and grinding are quite different operations. While you always grind into the edge, you must always buff off the edge. This is the major safety consideration—buffing into the edge could cause a kickback and send you to the emergency room to have a tool removed from your leg. (Another important safety consideration is to wear safety glasses when buffing.) You must also touch the surface you wish to buff tangentially to the wheel. This would be alternately the bevel and the back until all feather is removed and a polish is created at the cutting edge. Most beginners make the mistake of sticking the tool into the wheel at an obtuse angle, which is counterproductive. Our goal is to end up with a flat or slightly concave bevel leading to an edge that is free of feather. Buffing tangentially to the wheel accomplishes this, while buffing at an obtuse angle washes out the edge, rounding it over and leaving a bevel that is unpredictable.

As outlined earlier, a turning tool is cutting correctly when the bevel is rubbing and the edge is just attacking. When the bevel is washed out, or rounded over, the tool must be tipped up much higher for the edge to attack. At this point we are riding a very short unpredictable bevel and are left with no sense of feel over the process. A correctly sharpened tool with a contiguous flat or slightly concave bevel is a joy to use, giving the turner a feel for what is happening.

If you find that a tool constantly catches, always look first to sharpening and not to technique. Examine the edge carefully. Often a small portion of the edge will be dull while the rest is sharp. As you roll the tool it naturally catches when you get to the dull section. To avoid further frustration, go back to the grinder, stones and/or buffer and get the tool sharp. Turner, heal thyself! In the remaining part of this chapter I cover each turning tool and give precise guidelines on correct geometry. Spend the time to make your tool look exactly like my drawing, and you'll be off to a great start.

Tools for spindle turning

Whenever we cut wood that has grain running parallel to the bed of the lathe, we're spindle turning. In this section, we'll look in detail at the tools designed specifically for spindle turning: the roughing-out gouge, the spindle gouge and the chisels. You'll also use a cutoff tool and scrapers in spindle turning, but since these tools can be used for faceplate work as well they'll be covered in a section on dual-purpose tools at the end of the chapter (see pp. 94-97).

The roughing-out gouge

The roughing-out gouge is used primarily to bring square or odd-shaped work round. Although not one of the essential tools for general spindle turning, it's certainly a very handy tool to have if you've got a stack of square billets ready for a production turning job.

Traditionally, a roughing-out gouge was just a very large spindle gouge, ground square on the end rather than to a fingernail point. Since high-speed steel is difficult to forge, today's HSS version of this tool is a piece of flat stock bent into a U. If anything, this modern version works better because the corners are well out of the way and less likely to catch. Gouges are sized by the width of the flute; roughing-out gouges are commonly available in widths from ¾ in. to 1½ in.

Selecting turning tools

Turning tools are available in two materials: carbon steel and high-speed steel (HSS). Traditionally, all turning tools were made out of carbon steel, and although tools of this material are still widely available, tool manufacturers are increasingly switching to high-speed steel for their premium turning-tool lines. HSS tools are more expensive, but they hold an edge longer, thus requiring less frequent sharpening.

The great advantage of high-speed steel over carbon steel is that it has the quality of "hot hardness." Whereas carbon steel cannot be heated above 430°F without drawing the temper, high-speed steel maintains its hardness at much higher temperatures and is thus more immune from damage in the grinder due to burning and/or overheating.

If you're one of the lucky few for whom money is no object, I recommend that you buy all HSS turning tools. If, like most of us, you have to watch your budget, begin with carbon-steel tools or a mix of carbon steel and HSS and upgrade to HSS as your budget permits. Remember, generations of turners have produced wonderful results without the benefit of high-speed steel; with carbon-steel tools, you just have to be more careful not to overheat the metal during grinding.

The order in which I would build a set of HSS tools is as follows: spindle gouge, bowl gouge, parting tool, roughing-out gouge, skew chisel and, finally, scrapers. You can get by with a carbon-steel skew chisel since, barring calamity (i.e., an edge-first fall onto a concrete floor), it can be sharpened exclusively on stones. Similarly, you can easily make scrapers from any available piece of steel.

Premium tools are offered in two types: standard and long-and-strong. Standard tools are what we use every day, while the more robust long-and-strong tools are for heavy-duty faceplate work. You will need them only if you progress to large bowl turning. Finally, avoid commercial sets of tools, unless they are such a bargain you cannot pass them up. Sets tend to include only two or three tools you really need, and the rest eventually become expensive scrapers.

Starting set		Add as needed	
For spindle turning:	For faceplate turning:	For spindle turning:	For faceplate turning:
• ½-in. spindle gouge*	• ½-in. bowl gouge	• ¼-in. and ¾-in. spindle gouges	• ¼-in. or ⅜-in. bowl gouge
• 1-in. or 1¼-in. skew chisel*	• wider scrapers	• ⅜-in. bedan or beading- and-parting tool	• long-and-strong scrapers
• ⅛-in. diamond parting tool*		• ½-in. or ¾-in. skew chisel	
• ¾-in. to 1¼-in. roughing-out gouge		• ¹⁄₁₆-in. parting tool	
• small scrapers		• more scrapers	
*These are a bare minimum for beginning spindle turning.			

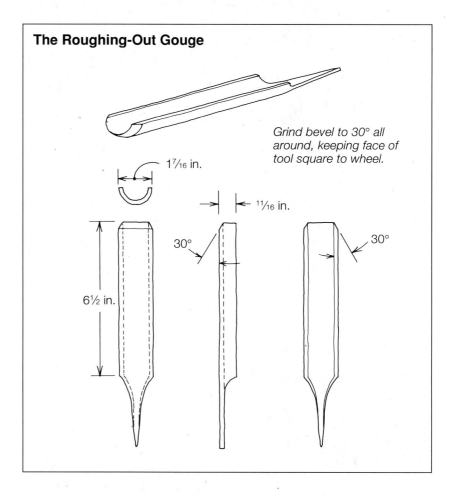

The Roughing-Out Gouge

Grind bevel to 30° all around, keeping face of tool square to wheel.

1^7/$_{16}$ in.

^{11}/$_{16}$ in.

6½ in.

30°

30°

Sharpening Straight from the factory, most roughing-out gouges tend to have too shallow a grind—somewhere around 50°—whereas it needs to be about 30°. To sharpen the gouge, start by grinding the face of the tool square, touching it at right angles to the wheel. Set the grinding rest to 30°, place the tool flat on the rest and roll it slowly from one corner to the other, keeping the face of the gouge square to the wheel. Once the bevel is ground to the correct angle, I usually give the edge a light buffing to remove feather and add a slight polish.

Use Roughing out is the act of bringing a square billet round, and for its intended use the roughing-out gouge is held at 90° to the axis of the work in a shear cut. Start the cut with the heel of the bevel rubbing, then slowly raise the tool until the full bevel rubs and the edge begins to cut. Because the work is square, your initial cuts will be interrupted—some of the time you'll be cutting the high spots, the rest of the time you'll be cutting air. The gouge can be difficult to control in an interrupted cut, so stand back a bit from the lathe and grip well back on the handle so that you have plenty of leverage. Use your

To turn a billet round, slide the roughing-out gouge laterally on the tool rest at 90° to the axis of the work.

Skew the gouge slightly to the left or right to turn a cylinder.

left hand over the gouge to hold firm pressure down on the rest. I like to hold my left index finger in the chip stream so the chips will be deflected away from my face.

As the gouge cuts, slide the tool laterally on the tool rest. Some turners roll the gouge from side to side as they work back and forth over the length of the work, but this does little more than distribute the wear more evenly over the cutting edge and thus lengthen the time between sharpenings.

Once the work is round, the gouge can be used for planing cylinders and gentle tapers (see pp. 98-102). For this operation, the gouge is best skewed slightly left or right according to the direction of travel. In this way, the bevel rides on the portion that has been cut, which tends to guide the tool. However, if the work becomes sufficiently thin for harmonic chatter to print out in the work (see pp. 110-114), then going back to 90° to the axis of the work will usually improve the finish. Under no circumstances should the roughing-out gouge be used in faceplate work because a potentially dangerous catch could result.

The spindle gouge

If I were exiled to a desert island with my lathe and allowed to bring only one tool, I'd choose the spindle gouge. The spindle gouge is designed for cutting coves, beads and other shapes in spindle turnings, but it can also be used to round rough billets and, in skilled hands, to perform some faceplate work. Mastery of the spindle gouge is the gateway to mastery of all turning tools.

Traditionally, spindle gouges were forged and somewhat more oval in section than the modern HSS gouges, which are made by milling a flute of standard radius in a length of round bar stock . While the traditional forged and modern HSS gouges work equally well, low-cost forged versions of the spindle gouge that have proliferated in recent years are of dubious quality. Some of these are so thin of section and/or flat in profile as to be unusable as spindle gouges, though they do make acceptable roughing gouges. A modern low-profile gouge is shown at right in the photo below.

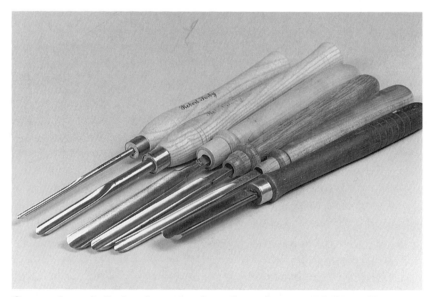

Gouges for spindle turning come in various shapes and sizes. Shown from left to right are two Sorby high-speed-steel spindle gouges, three traditional forged gouges (made by Buck Brothers in the 1920s) and a modern, low-cost, low-profile gouge.

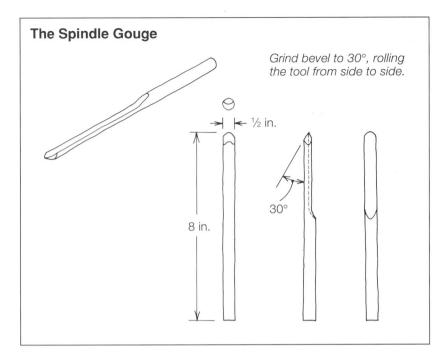

The Spindle Gouge

Grind bevel to 30°, rolling the tool from side to side.

½ in.

8 in.

30°

Spindle gouges are commonly available in ¼-in., ⅜-in. and ½-in. sizes. The ½-in. gouge is probably the most generally useful, while the smaller widths are handy for fine work. Wider spindle gouges (up to 1 in.) are sold for large furniture turnings and architectural work.

Sharpening   The spindle gouge is more difficult to grind than most turning tools because it has a convex curved edge and the standard rest on the grinder can be used only at the very center of the bevel. To overcome this problem, it's best to use a round bar-type rest (see pp. 69-70), which allows you to roll the tool on the wheel while simultaneously tipping it upward.

Start with the gouge at 90° to the grinder, contacting the very center of the bevel to the very center of the wheel at the desired 30° angle, as shown in the top photo on p. 84. To grind the left side of the bevel, roll the tool to the left while simultaneously swinging the handle to the left and pushing the tool forward and to the right. You finish with the tool rolled over to the left, with the bevel to the right of and higher on the wheel than where you started (see the bottom photo on p. 84). Now go back to the center of the tool and grind the right side. Once the tool is correctly ground, hone the edge on the buffer.

To grind a spindle gouge, start with the center of the bevel at 90° to the center of the wheel face (at left). Grind the left side of the bevel by rolling the tool to the left while tipping it upward and angling it to the right (below). Do just the opposite to grind the right side.

The shape of the fingernail grind on a spindle gouge is a matter of personal preference. I like to use a long, tapered grind (what I call a "high-society" grind), while my friend and fellow turning-author Michael Dunbar prefers a blunt "working man's" fingernail grind.

Use The correct way to use a spindle gouge is to hold the tool at 90° to the axis of the work with the bevel rubbing and the edge just cutting. This is the classic shear cut, as shown in the drawing on p. 67. While this drawing assumes that we're cutting a round cylinder, in reality we're usually cutting complex shapes, such as coves and beads. In such complex cuts the gouge has to be simultaneously rolled side to side, angled left or right, and slid in and out on the tool rest. This movement of the gouge is all with the idea of obeying what I call the "Law of Perpendiculars," as shown in the drawing below. According to this law, a perpendicular rising out of the spindle gouge should coincide with any perpendicular constructed from the surface of the work. If we're obeying the law of perpendiculars to the letter, just the very point of the spindle gouge is cutting. Unfortunately our two-dimensional drawing does not tell the whole story.

The first impression is that we merely need to roll the tool to obey the law. However, we must also keep the bevel rubbing if we're to avoid a catch. To do this, the tool must be angled left or right and slid a bit forward or back during the roll. We'll learn much more about using the spindle gouge to make complex cuts in Chapter 4.

The spindle gouge must be rolled, angled left or right and slid back and forth depending on the intended cut. Shown here are shear cuts on a cylinder (top) and at the top edge of a cove (above).

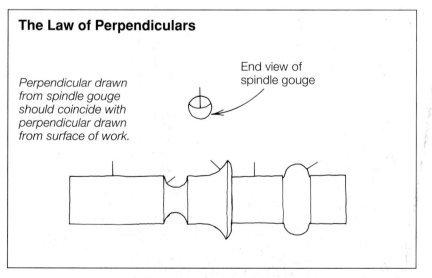

The Law of Perpendiculars

Perpendicular drawn from spindle gouge should coincide with perpendicular drawn from surface of work.

End view of spindle gouge

The skew chisel

The skew chisel is a step in the evolutionary chain of a group of tools loosely called chisels. Unlike regular woodworking chisels, the skew has a bevel on both the top and bottom side, and the cutting edge is not square to the shank. Double-beveled chisels with a square cutting edge were common in England years ago, and some turners still use them. For this square-edged tool to work, it had to be angled, or "skewed," 15° to 20° in the direction of the cut. Early toolmakers realized that they could skew the edge the same amount and achieve a longer cutting edge from the same blank of steel, and so the skew chisel was born. The tool no longer had to be skewed to the work and so was more natural to use.

The right amount to skew the edge is 15° to 20°. Makers of economy sets often skew the edge as much as 45°, and such tools do not work as well. Skew chisels are sold in ½-in., ¾-in., 1-in. and 1¼-in. sizes. The larger two sizes are best for beginners to learn with.

Sharpening   The two bevels of the skew chisel should meet at an included angle of about 42°. As outlined in the honing section (see pp. 73-74), a skew chisel works best with flat bevels so it should be sharpened only on whetstones (I'd use a grinder only if I'd dropped a skew edge-down onto a concrete floor). Removing the tool handle during whetting greatly aids in feeling and holding a flat bevel.

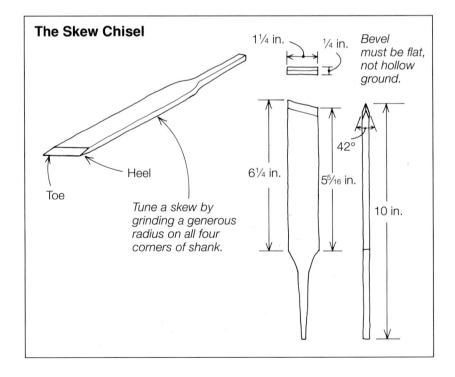

The Skew Chisel

1¼ in.

¼ in.

Bevel must be flat, not hollow ground.

Heel

Toe

Tune a skew by grinding a generous radius on all four corners of shank.

6¼ in.

5⁵⁄₁₆ in.

42°

10 in.

A skew will benefit from a bit of tuning. I like to grind a generous radius on the four corners of the shank, which allows the tool to slide and roll more smoothly on the tool rest. Rounding the corners also moves the center of gravity toward the center a marginal amount (see the sidebar on oval and round skews on p. 88). I buff the ground radius with emery compound followed by stainless-steel compound to bring the entire shank up to a high polish. (I buff the shanks of all my tools.)

Use The skew chisel is one of the toughest turning tools to master. I think of using a skew as akin to falconry. Good falcons are taken as young adults and taught to tolerate humans. Each time the falconer flies the bird there is a chance that it will return and bite its master. Most of the time, however, there is a beautiful symbiotic relationship, which results in meat for man and beast.

So it is with the skew. Used properly, the results are fast and magnificent—the tool is fun to use. Even in the best of hands, however, the tool will suddenly turn on the turner and bite unmercifully.

To start a cut with the skew, place the corner of the shank on the tool rest and the heel of the bevel on the work. Tip the tool downward onto the bevel until it just starts to cut. Normal cutting should take place on about one-third of the cutting edge on line AA, as shown in the drawing below. As you approach a shoulder (when cutting up to a bead, for example), the tool must be slid forward on the rest so that cutting takes place on the very heel, as shown in the drawing. Although the drawing shows the tool at right angles to the work, in

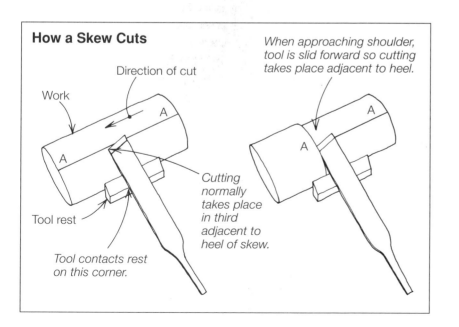

How a Skew Cuts

Direction of cut

Work

When approaching shoulder, tool is slid forward so cutting takes place adjacent to heel.

A

A

A

Tool rest

Cutting normally takes place in third adjacent to heel of skew.

Tool contacts rest on this corner.

The taming of the skew

The latest development in the evolution of the skew chisel is a skew available from Sorby (see Sources of Supply on pp. 191-192) that is oval rather than rectangular in cross section. There is also a simple device called a Stabilax that can be attached to any skew to achieve the same end as the Sorby tool. Both the Sorby oval skew and the Stabilax will tame a skew in the clumsiest of hands.

The reason a flat skew chisel is so difficult to use is that the tool is unbalanced. The center of gravity is not under the downward moments of force, because, of necessity, only one edge of the tool can contact the rest during turning. While grinding the sharp corners along the shank (see p. 87) helps somewhat, using the Stabilax or a Sorby oval skew allows much greater control. Both have a center of gravity that's more nearly under the center of force—a center of gravity that's free to change with the rolling action of the tool.

I was introduced to the Stabilax at a Los Angeles woodworking show by its inventor, Richard Lukes. He offered me one to try out. As I stepped up to the lathe with the Stabilax bolted to my skew, I was very skeptical of what I took to be just another woodworking gimmick. The first few sample straight cuts didn't

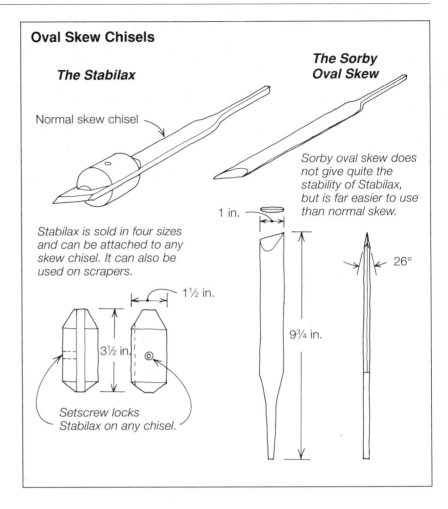

Oval Skew Chisels

The Stabilax

The Sorby Oval Skew

Normal skew chisel

Sorby oval skew does not give quite the stability of Stabilax, but is far easier to use than normal skew.

Stabilax is sold in four sizes and can be attached to any skew chisel. It can also be used on scrapers.

1 in.

1½ in.

3½ in.

9¾ in.

26°

Setscrew locks Stabilax on any chisel.

really seem all that different from using a plain old skew. The eye-opener came when I started to cut some coves and beads. I was truly amazed. It got to the point where I was doing things to invite a catch and really had to work to get one.

My children (then aged 8 and 10) were at the show too, and I decided to press them into service to test the Stabilax further. They had been turning for some time, but not yet with the skew. Using the Stabilax,

they took to the skew like ducks to water and could duplicate anything I asked them to, with no idea that a skew should be difficult to use.

There has to be a down side to everything, and so it is with the Stabilax. I frequently use the toe of a skew to cut accent lines or lay out beads, and a large skew fitted with the Stabilax tends to be a bit clunky for getting into tight places.

reality it is usually angled a few degrees in the direction of travel. Angling the tool brings the heel and toe farther away from causing a catch and clears the side of the tool at a shoulder. In no circumstances should cutting take place in the proximity of the toe or a catch will result.

Skews are very good for cutting cylinders, gentle curves and tapers (see p. 102), and they leave a finish unmatched by any other turning tool. In skilled hands, it's even possible to use the skew chisel to cut beads. As long as the bevel is kept rubbing, the skew behaves beautifully, but if you lift off the bevel for even an instant, the edge will dig in and start generating a screw thread on the work. The toe will ride backward and dig in, causing a nasty catch.

You should never use the skew chisel for faceplate work (other than cutting small detail lines with the point of the toe). If used in the normal way in faceplate work, the tool will catch and possibly rip the work from the faceplate or break the tool handle.

Beading-and-parting tool and the bedan

The beading-and-parting tool is simply a narrow, traditional woodturner's chisel. Like the skew chisel, it has a double bevel ground to about 42°, but the end is square, not skewed. The bedan differs from the beading-and-parting tool only in that it has a single bevel ground to 30°. Both tools are available in fairly narrow sizes, generally around 3⁄8 in.

The beading-and-parting tool and the bedan are sharpened on stones, just like skew chisels (see pp. 74-75). Some turners, especially in England, use both these tools to roll beads, but I feel that they're better suited for sizing tenons (see p. 117). Since a bedan is very similar to a regular carpenter's chisel, I have always used one of the latter for this purpose. Beading-and-parting tools and bedans can also be used to size an area of a turning with calipers for duplication (see pp. 115-116).

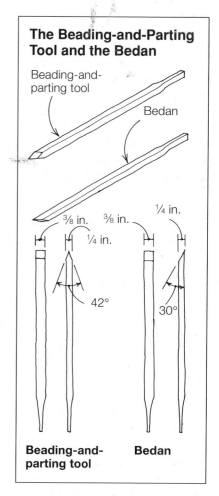

The Beading-and-Parting Tool and the Bedan

Beading-and-parting tool

Bedan

3⁄8 in. 3⁄8 in. 1⁄4 in.

1⁄4 in.

42° 30°

Beading-and-parting tool   Bedan

Tools for faceplate turning

In faceplate work, the grain of the work runs at right angles to the axis of the lathe. For every rotation of the work we are cutting against the grain half the time. If we use any spindle tool in a classic shear cut (as shown in the drawing on p. 67), it will dig in when we go against the grain and result in a catch. In spindle turning, we are presented with a uniform grain structure that makes riding the bevel predictable. In face work, we don't have this luxury and the wood is essentially softer to the tool's way of thinking when we go against the grain. To overcome this problem, we need to use a tool for faceplate work that cuts in a totally different manner. This tool is the bowl gouge.

The bowl gouge

Like the spindle gouge, the bowl gouge was traditionally forged, and its body looks quite different from today's high-speed-steel version, which is made by milling an elliptical flute in a piece of round bar stock (see the photo below). Close inspection, however, reveals that the forged gouge and the milled gouge are almost identical at the business end. The difference between the bowl gouge and the spindle gouge is the shape of the flute. The bowl gouge has a much deeper U-shaped flute, while the spindle gouge has a shallow flute of constant radius. Depending on the manufacturer the flute can be anything from a deep U to a complex parabolic curve (see the drawing on p. 92).

Bowl gouges are sold in ¼-in., ⅜-in. and ½-in. sizes. If you're just learning to faceplate turn I'd recommend starting with a ½-in. gouge and adding a ¼-in. gouge if necessary later.

Today's high-speed-steel bowl gouges are milled from round bar stock (top). Traditional gouges were forged from carbon steel (bottom). Although the shanks are different in cross section, the cutting edges are virtually identical.

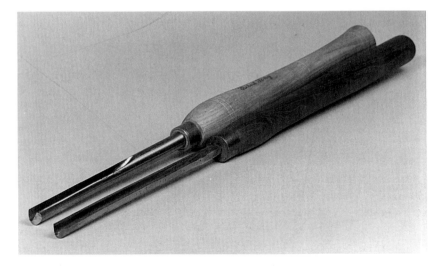

Start to grind the bowl gouge with one corner against the wheel at the required angle (above). Roll the gouge toward the center, raising the handle as you work (above right). Take the tool off the wheel when you reach the nose (right), then repeat the procedure on the opposite corner.

Sharpening The bowl gouge is one of the toughest tools to sharpen, because the grind is asymmetrical. It has a shallow grind on the nose that grows progressively more severe toward the corners. What we should aim for is about 60° to 70° of grind on the nose (some turners quote the complementary angle of 20° to 30°, which is technically the clearance) with about 30° to 40° at the top of the corners.

As when grinding any gouge, it's best to use a bar rest in the grinder when sharpening a bowl gouge. The grinding process begins on one of the corners. Place the side bevel against the wheel at the required 30° to 40° angle, as shown in the top left photo. Once you've ground to an edge, start rolling the tool toward the center, while simultaneously lifting the handle. You should end up at the very nose with the requisite 60° to 70° grind in that area (top right photo). Now go to the opposite corner and execute a mirror image of the first maneuver. The idea is for both operations to meet perfectly at the tip of the nose. A bowl gouge seldom needs honing, because the end grain of the workpiece quickly de-burrs the edge, but it will require frequent sharpening. For a finish cut with a bowl gouge, a light buffing can be helpful.

I've observed that most beginners try to sharpen the bowl gouge by grinding parallel to the cutting edge, which is absolutely the wrong approach. If ground correctly, the tool should have a hollow grind with each grind mark at right angles to the cutting edge. You can buy a jig for sharpening bowl gouges, but these don't work out too well because the grind of the tool is asymmetrical and is often modified a bit, depending on the job. For example, the nose is ground flatter for deep vessels turned through a narrow mouth opening.

Bowl gouges typically come from the factory with a square face and a uniform grind all the way round. The drawing below shows a good general-purpose grind that modifies the factory grind a little. This modified grind slants the face back about 15° and thus gets the corners out of the way. It's a friendly, "catch-resistant" formula that will

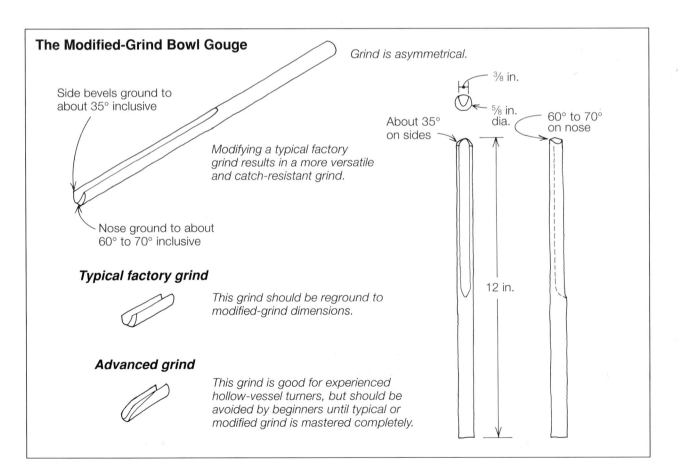

The Modified-Grind Bowl Gouge

Grind is asymmetrical.

Side bevels ground to about 35° inclusive

Modifying a typical factory grind results in a more versatile and catch-resistant grind.

Nose ground to about 60° to 70° inclusive

³⁄₈ in.

⁵⁄₈ in. dia.

60° to 70° on nose

About 35° on sides

12 in.

Typical factory grind

This grind should be reground to modified-grind dimensions.

Advanced grind

This grind is good for experienced hollow-vessel turners, but should be avoided by beginners until typical or modified grind is mastered completely.

cover most faceplate situations encountered in general woodworking. If the gouge should catch, the modified grind tends to allow the tool to roll out of trouble and so prevent further catching.

Many experienced bowl turners make a very long grind by raking one or both corners back considerably. Although this advanced grind improves surface finish, it can catch unmercifully and may be dangerous in the hands of a beginner. Learn to use the modified grind well before experimenting.

Use   The secret to the bowl gouge is that instead of cutting directly on the periphery of the work, it cuts sideways. Normal cutting creates a step in the work, and the bottom bevel of the tool cuts away the face of this step. In this way the nose is rubbing on the area previously cut, which prevents the tool from being drawn in when it goes against the grain. The drawing below shows the bowl gouge making a right-hand cut away from the headstock. Swinging the handle left or right controls the depth of cut, that is, the height of the ledge. Rotating the handle left or right controls the quality of the cut made by the bottom bevel on the face of the ledge. Rotate the gouge until the bevel is rubbing, holding the tool fairly level and about on the centerline of the work. When cutting perfectly, the nose bevel is rubbing on the surface previously cut and the lower bevel is rubbing on the face of the ledge. Cutting to the left is a mirror image of the cut shown in the drawing.

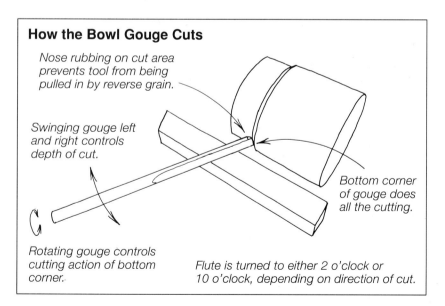

How the Bowl Gouge Cuts

Nose rubbing on cut area prevents tool from being pulled in by reverse grain.

Swinging gouge left and right controls depth of cut.

Bottom corner of gouge does all the cutting.

Rotating gouge controls cutting action of bottom corner.

Flute is turned to either 2 o'clock or 10 o'clock, depending on direction of cut.

In a pinch, you can use a spindle gouge for face work. To do so, you first have to grind a much shorter bevel on the tool—about 50° to 60°. The tool is then used in a sideways cut rather than a straight-on paring cut. Many turners advocate the so-called multi-purpose gouge, which is a long-and-strong spindle gouge ground to a compromise between the needs of spindle turning and faceplate turning. It's used in the normal way for spindle work, but does not yield quite the surface quality of a true spindle grind. It may readily be used for face work by cutting sideways.

Dual-purpose tools

The tools we have considered thus far are, for the most part, task-specific. Now let's turn our attention to those tools that are designed for use with either spindle turning or face work. In this category are the cutoff or parting tool and an infinite variety of scrapers.

The cutoff or parting tool

The terms "cutoff" and "parting" are interchangeable, and as both names imply this tool is used to cut work away from the lathe. There are three variations of the tool, as shown in the drawing at left. The economy model is simply a flat, rectangular section ground with two bevels at about a 50° angle that meet to form the cutting edge. It can easily be made from an old file.

The second design, which is the one I prefer to use, is the diamond-section parting tool. Because the edges of the tool are relieved, there is less friction when working a deep kerf with the diamond-section tool than with the economy model. In addition, the diamond-section tool can cut a much narrower kerf when cutting into the face of face-plate work. In this situation the tool is parallel to the lathe bed and the cutoff kerf is a circle. The third type of cutoff tool is available only from Sorby (see Sources of Supply on pp. 191-192) in high-speed steel and is called a fluted parting tool. It gives only marginally better performance than the diamond-section tool and has the disadvantage that it scores tool rests.

Parting tools are available in $1/16$-in., $1/8$-in., $3/16$-in. and $1/4$-in. sizes. The $1/8$-in. tool is a good starting size, and you may want to add a $1/16$-in. model for small work. I've had no need to use the wider parting tools since a bedan or beading-and-parting tool can do the job just as well.

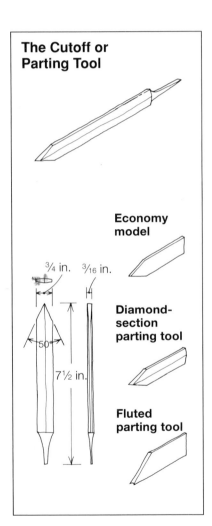

The Cutoff or Parting Tool

Economy model

3/4 in.   3/16 in.

Diamond-section parting tool

50°

7½ in.

Fluted parting tool

With the heel of the bottom bevel against the work, rock the parting tool down and forward until the work is cut through. The operator's left hand supports and catches the cutoff.

Sharpening   All three types of parting tool are ground to about a 50° angle, although the fluted model has only one bevel. Parting tools lend themselves well to the flat grinding rest. Place the edge of the shank on the rest (which should be set at about 25°) and slide the tool forward until the bevel contacts the wheel. Turn the tool over and repeat until an edge is formed. Take some care to keep the edge in the center of the tool, especially with the diamond-section tool. Honing a parting tool is seldom necessary, but it can never hurt.

Use   Place the edge of the parting tool on the rest and the heel of the bottom bevel on the work. Slide the tool back on the rest until the bevel rubs and the edge starts cutting. Now rock the tool down on the rest (raising the handle) and slide forward as necessary until the work is parted in two. If the work starts to bind against the edges of the tool, make overlapping strokes to keep the kerf wider than the tool. I usually bring my left hand around to support and catch the work as it comes free.

For the fluted parting tool, the process is much the same except that the fluted edge is placed on the rest and there is no bevel to start. Simply apply the tool at a tangent to the surface of the work and rock downward and slide forward, as with the diamond-section tool. Whichever parting tool you use, you should aim to end up dead on-center as the piece drops away.

When turning heavier work, it's best to plan the cutoff at the head-stock end of the lathe. This way the work falls free and is disconnected from the power. For small, light spindles, you can safely make the cut-off anywhere on the piece.

Scrapers

For all my harping on the importance of using shear-cutting techniques, there are times when using a scraper is the only way a cut can be made. I use scrapers for very small beads, undercuts and difficult interrupted cuts, to name but a few applications.

The term "scraper" refers to a whole class of tools that are purposely sharpened to a burr and used at a downhill slant. I have shown only two scrapers in the drawing at left, but you'll probably end up with many more. Tool suppliers offer a large selection of scrapers, but they're something you can just as easily make yourself. A scraper is very much a tool of the moment, so feel free to improvise. Almost any piece of steel will work as a scraper, especially if you are making just a one-time quick cut. I have sharpened old screwdrivers, files and pieces of car spring to improvise scrapers. You can use the scraper for one job then regrind it to a new shape for the next. If you have a problem that a gouge won't solve, a scraper is often the answer.

Sharpening   There are two ways to sharpen a scraper: grinding and burnishing. Most commercial scrapers (and this includes all high-speed-steel scrapers) are too hard to burnish, so they must be ground. Grinding a scraper is simplicity itself. Set the grinding rest so that the bevel will be ground to about a 75° inclusive angle (most turners refer to this as 15° of clearance in the edge). Place the tool flat on the rest, push it into the wheel and grind until a burr is formed. (A burr is the natural outcome any time a tool is ground.) Keeping firm pressure on the tool, swing the tool to achieve the desired radius. Many students seem to think that you need to grind the tool upside down to raise the burr, but it forms just as well grinding right side up and it is much easier to concentrate on the shape of the edge.

Burnishing a scraper will work only if the tool is soft enough, which eliminates virtually all commercially available scrapers. With carbon-steel tools, the technique is identical to sharpening a cabinet scraper, and, in my opinion, it produces a better burr than grinding. To burnish a scraper, first file the bevel to the desired angle, then use whetstones to bring the bevel and the back to a good finish. Now take a burnisher, which is simply a round or oval-shaped bar of very hard, polished steel, and rub it firmly along the bevel edge. By slanting the burnisher toward the back of the tool, a burr is rolled.

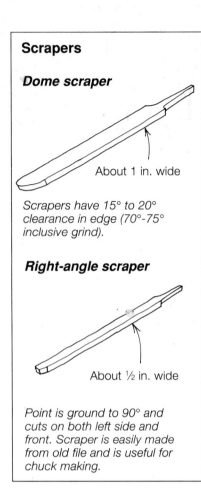

Scrapers

Dome scraper

About 1 in. wide

Scrapers have 15° to 20° clearance in edge (70°-75° inclusive grind).

Right-angle scraper

About ½ in. wide

Point is ground to 90° and cuts on both left side and front. Scraper is easily made from old file and is useful for chuck making.

Use A scraper is always used downhill, so that the burr can attack (see the photo at right). Although you might think that we're taking a negative rake cut, we're really taking a highly positive one. The tool works exactly the same as a cabinet scraper, and it is the burr that does the cutting, not the bevel. The short length of the burr effectively limits the depth of cut per revolution of the work, making it a safe, predictable tool.

In face work, scrapers should be used with a very light touch or they will tear in the reverse grain areas. Once they do, a gouge or extensive sanding is the only thing that will remove the blemish. Scrapers work very well in plank grain or pure end grain such as that encountered at the end of a spindle turning. An arm rest (see the sidebar below) is a handy accessory for supporting a scraper in such situations.

Scrapers make the cut with the tool angled downhill.

The arm rest

The arm rest is an auxiliary tool rest that saves you from having to move your main tool rest when working on the face of the work. The first time I saw an arm rest was in the hands of fourth-generation master turner Dick Bailey. It struck me as such a good idea that I went home and made one myself. You'll also have to make one (or have a blacksmith make one for you), since I know none that are available commercially. I've given sizes to follow in the drawing.

To use the arm rest, place its handle under your left arm and the shank on the tool rest. Then set your turning tool in the hook

of the arm rest and control it with your right hand. The arm rest is most often used with scrapers for making chucks. (It should not be used with gouges or skew chisels.) An added advantage of the arm rest is that it allows you to obtain instant

center height for the tool. At the very center of the work the tool must be exactly on center, and any inaccuracies can be corrected by raising or lowering your shoulder. You can see the arm rest in action in the photo on p. 52.

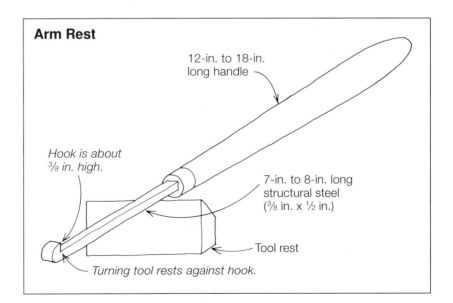

Arm Rest

12-in. to 18-in. long handle

Hook is about ⅜ in. high.

7-in. to 8-in. long structural steel (⅜ in. x ½ in.)

Tool rest

Turning tool rests against hook.

CHAPTER 4
Turning Techniques

Now that we've looked at ways of holding work in the lathe and sharpening and using tools, it's time to get down to the actual mechanics of turning. I'm going to cover techniques according to how frequently they're encountered in making furniture—from the tasks necessary in most turnings to practices you may never use. This will lead us in a natural progression, and make this chapter a ready source of reference for solving turning problems. Along the way, we'll also look at the processes of duplication, sanding and finishing. Let's begin with turning a simple cylinder.

Cylinders, tapers and gentle curves

To create a spindle turning we start by turning a rough billet round and then cut design elements composed of coves and beads (see pp. 102-109) into the surface of the cylinder. These design elements are often connected by tapers and gentle curves.

The best tool for turning a rough billet round is the roughing-out gouge (see pp. 78-82). To begin roughing out, present the heel of the bevel to the spinning work. Because the work isn't round, only the

Cutting a bead is a basic spindle-turning technique.

corners will contact the gouge initially, making a click, click, click sound. Rock the tool down until it just starts to cut, then slide the gouge laterally back and forth on the rest to bring the work round.

In the initial stage of turning, the gouge is presented at 90° to the work, but as the billet becomes round the tool should be skewed a bit left or right to achieve a more accurate cylinder. Knowing when the work is truly round is something that comes with experience, and it's better found by touch rather than by stopping and starting the lathe to inspect the billet. Touching the back of the roughing-out gouge (just behind the bevel) is a good test for roundness—you will hear a clicking sound from any flat spots. I prefer simply to touch the back of the spinning work across from the tool rest to feel for any surface imperfection. You should also learn to read the "ghost," which is the hard-to-distinguish pattern created by the corners of the work spinning in the

Selecting wood for turning

Any wood can be turned, but some species turn much better than others. Generally speaking, any wood that's valued for furniture construction will also be excellent for turning, including maple, cherry, mahogany, walnut and oak. Of the North American woods that are widely available commercially, maple is always a sure winner. It is most forgiving of mistakes, and cut correctly, it produces superlative finishes. Although pine and poplar respond well to shear-cutting techniques, it's more difficult to produce a high-level finish on these woods. They're woods to use when some mastery of turning has been gained, or for practice.

A turning billet with checks or defects (right) should be discarded.

For furniture construction, select clear, sound planks, preferably quartersawn. Discard any billets that show signs of defects. It's also best to saw 2 in. to 4 in. off the end of a plank, because there is invariably some checking in this area and it's often hard to notice. Finding such checks is frustrating when your turning is nearly completed. For work that's going to be turned over its entire length, the plank may be left rough and simply ripped to an approximate square of the desired size. Since you're going to turn the entire length there's no sense in

A roughing-out gouge is the best tool to use to turn a square billet round.

wasting time with planing. For turnings where a portion is to be left square (such as for a table leg), taking the time to joint and plane to a perfect square before turning is important. It's equally important to find the exact center for precise chucking. To find the center, draw lines that connect the corners on the end of the billet; making a light mark with a center punch will also aid in centering the billet on the lathe.

Turning green wood

Until the early 19th century, it was standard practice to turn green wood (the wood of a freshly fallen tree). I always have my students do some work on green stock because it builds confidence and because green wood is relatively inexpensive. Although you might expect the wood to check as it dries, it will do so only if there is a complete annual ring in the billet. The turning will become slightly oval as it dries, but not so you can notice visually. You'll be able to feel the eccentricity, and this is a hallmark of a pre-Machine-Age turning.

Green-wood billets should be cut from freshly fallen, deep-forest trees with straight, clear sections of trunk. Saw a section to the desired length and rive (split) it into billets, using a wedge to start and then a froe. A cardinal rule when riving is always to split the wood in equal pieces (that is, cut halves first, then quarters, then eighths; never halves to eighths). Otherwise, the split will walk in the direction of the smaller piece. Once a billet of the desired size is obtained, it can be further refined with a draw knife before it's mounted in the lathe. One great advantage of using riven stock is that all grain fibers in the billet are parallel, which allows you to turn chair legs of much daintier proportion than you could with dry, resawn wood.

Bowls can also be turned from green wood. Chainsaw a blank of suitable size from a fresh log, making sure not to include a complete annual ring in the blank. Mount the blank on the lathe as explained on pp. 39-42, and faceplate-turn in the normal way. The bowl will warp as it dries, but that will only add to its charm. Some turners blank the bowl to rough shape, but with a heavy wall (about $\frac{1}{10}$ the diameter). They then allow the blank to dry for at least three months, then turn it to a finished bowl with a thinner wall. The reward of using green wood is a much larger, deeper bowl than is possible with kiln-dried wood.

Once in the lathe, green wood is a joy to turn. Long, continuous shavings peel off the blank, and the finish is superlative. Expect to be sprayed with some water, and don't leave shavings on the lathe or rust will be sure to follow.

lathe before it is round. Good lighting plays an important role in helping you see the ghost, but careful observation will enable you to see the final diameter.

Although the roughing-out gouge will leave a very good finish when angled slightly left or right, a better cylinder with a better finish can usually be obtained by switching to the skew chisel for the final stages of the cylinder. For information on turning a cylinder with a skew, see pp. 86-89.

Cutting a taper or a gentle curve is much the same technique as cutting a cylinder. Again, a roughing-out gouge is a good tool for this task. Anywhere a taper or gentle curve meets a design element, such as a bead, a hard edge is encountered. At such areas you'll have to switch from the roughing-out gouge to the spindle gouge to cut up to the hard edge. The spindle gouge is used in nearly a sideways cut, stopping just at the edge. It's helpful to nick the edge first with the toe of a skew chisel.

As with cutting cylinders, for the best results with gentle curves and tapers you should use the skew. A wide skew chisel (1 in. or more) used in a shear cut leaves a better surface finish, cuts a more consistent taper or gentle curve and can be used right up to a shoulder. Slight inconsistencies in work diameter are common when using gouges. Although they can be largely overcome by using a roughing-out gouge in a sideways cut, a skew by design handily overcomes the problem.

Use of the skew in a shear cut is described on p. 87. The main thing to remember is to keep the cut in about one-third of the cutting edge nearest the heel, as shown in the drawing on p. 87. Because the edge of the skew is effectively the tangent to a circle, the width of the skew must be scaled to the work. Large-diameter work requires a wider chisel so that the corners can clear the surface without catching. As you approach a shoulder, you must slide the skew forward slightly so that cutting takes place at and adjacent to the heel.

Coves and beads

All spindle-turning shapes encompass the turning of either the cove or the bead, and mastering these two shapes will allow you to turn virtually any furniture spindle. Coves and beads are like compulsory figures in skating—you can never practice them enough. Let's start with the cove, which can be cut only with the spindle gouge.

Cutting the cove

In its simplest form, a cove is a U cut down into the surface of a cylinder. The key to cutting any cove is to obey the Law of Perpendiculars (see p. 85); the drawing below of a simple cove, with perpendiculars constructed at three points, illustrates the theory.

The idea is to start at the top edges of the cove and take a series of scooping cuts, always ending at the exact bottom. Start at the left edge of the cove with the gouge almost on its side and the flute pointing toward the center of the cove (see the drawing on p. 104). Bring the gouge to the center of the cove, rolling it to horizontal as the cut progresses. Now repeat the motion from the right edge of the cove. Take a series of scooping cuts from each side until the cove is cut to the desired profile. Always cut downhill from the larger diameter to the smaller, and don't cut beyond the center of the cove bottom.

Rolling the gouge as the cut progresses is only part of the story. In addition to rolling, the tool must be angled left or right and slid slightly forward to keep the bevel rubbing. A common mistake among beginners is to lock the handle of the gouge in one position against the hip and simply roll the tool in the prescribed manner. A catch is always the result since the cove cut is not as simple as it seems. You're actually cutting a complicated compound shape, and if you simply roll the tool

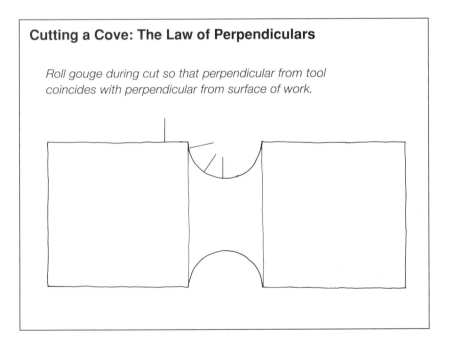

Cutting a Cove: The Law of Perpendiculars

Roll gouge during cut so that perpendicular from tool coincides with perpendicular from surface of work.

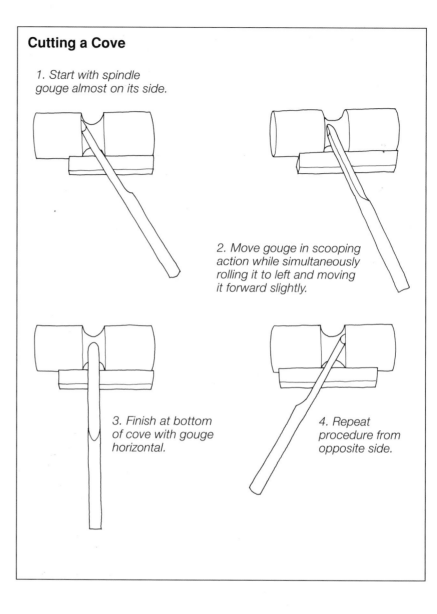

Cutting a Cove

1. Start with spindle gouge almost on its side.

2. Move gouge in scooping action while simultaneously rolling it to left and moving it forward slightly.

3. Finish at bottom of cove with gouge horizontal.

4. Repeat procedure from opposite side.

you don't keep the bevel rubbing. The drawing above shows the correct tool alignment. Pay particular attention to the handle and the large amount of left, right and up-and-down movement required.

The most frequent mistakes when cutting a cove are failure to roll the gouge sufficiently (it should start almost on its side) and failure to angle the tool left or right sufficiently to have the bevel rubbing at the start of the cut. The tool must also be slid very slightly forward as the cut progresses because the diameter of the billet at the cove is getting smaller, so the tangent point to the surface is moving away from the tool rest.

Another common mistake is using a gouge that is too wide for the cove. The cove *must* be wider than the gouge. Thus it's useful to have a range of spindle gouges for cutting different-size coves. I try to use a gouge that's about three-quarters the size of the cove I plan to cut.

Cutting the bead

The bead is the opposite of the cove, both in shape and in the way it is turned. It can be cut with either the gouge or a chisel (skew, bedan or beading-and-parting tool). Although it's exciting to cut beads with the skew, the gouge is much better suited for beginners. Cutting a bead with a spindle gouge is simple and straightforward, whereas using a chisel requires a precise sense of being flat on the bevel. As a woodworker, I find that my turning is done in spurts when I need parts, and there are usually long lulls between sessions. After such a hiatus it takes an hour of so of turning for my skills to return. During this acclimatization period I'm hard pressed to turn a bead with a skew and frequently catch, though once I'm back in the groove again it's a simple matter. Therefore, the only beads I cut with a skew are during turning demonstrations to show others how to do it.

When making furniture, whether professionally or for your own pleasure, time is money. You're dealing with expensive billets of wood that took time to prepare, and you can't afford to waste them. A catch with a chisel is a catastrophic event that generally relegates the work to the firewood pile. Even if this only happens once in every six or eight pieces, it's still a great waste. You save time and money by taking the time to reach for the gouge. Therefore I strongly recommend that the gouge be used exclusively for cutting beads. Not only will you cut a cleaner bead of better profile, but you'll also have a better rate of success. Reserve the skew for planing cylinders and gentle tapers.

The first task in cutting a bead is laying it out. Experience will allow you to draw two pencil lines to mark the width of the bead, then proceed to cut it directly into the surface of a cylinder. At first, you're better off using the toe of a skew chisel to demarcate the limits of the bead. While a bead can now be cut directly into the surface of the cylinder, it's a good idea for beginners to cut away the area on either side to leave a raised square ridge, properly called a "rondel." Raising a rondel first allows you to cut your bead without the worry of the bottom edge of the gouge catching on the adjoining surfaces. To raise the rondel, use the toe of a skew chisel as described for turning square to round with a shoulder (see pp. 109-110).

A good way to learn to cut beads is to start by cutting a raised ridge above the surface of the cylinder, properly called a 'rondel.'

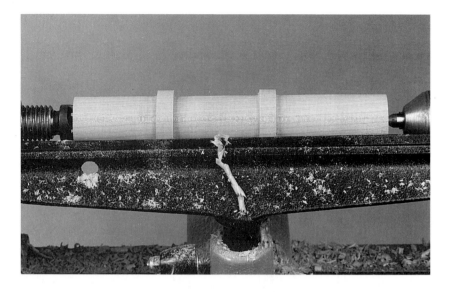

Whether you're starting with a rondel or cutting directly into the surface of a cylinder, start in the middle of the bead in a classic shear cut, with the gouge held at 90° to the axis of the lathe and the flute facing up (as shown in the drawing on on the facing page and the photos on pp. 108-109). If you're cutting into the surface directly, you'll have to open up the areas adjacent to the bead slightly. To cut the left side of the bead, angle the tool left, slide it back slightly on the tool rest and roll it in the direction of the cut. Now raise the handle until the tool is on its side and aimed at the center of the work. (The tool is now aligned with a radius of the work.) Push forward until you reach the bottom of the bead. As the cut progresses you'll have to swing the handle around behind the tool to create the curve of the bead and keep the bevel rubbing.

Most beginners fail to lift the handle high enough or roll the tool exactly on its side at the final stage of the cut. With the tool rolled only 45° and the handle raised only slightly, the result is invariably a catch on the adjoining surfaces.

To cut the right side of the bead, return to the center and reverse the procedure. Most beginners have difficulty making both halves of a bead symmetrical, but this comes with practice. The nice thing about using a gouge is that you can easily fine-tune a lopsided bead by recutting it by halves. Although you can do the same thing with a skew, it's much more difficult to produce a bead with a flowing profile.

Cutting a Bead

Normal view (standing at the lathe)

1. Start at top center of bead in normal shear cut.

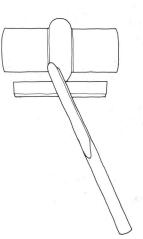

2. Roll tool and angle left, cutting downhill.

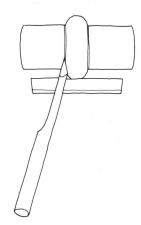

3. End with tool rolled sideways and pointing at center of work.

Front view (at tool-rest level)

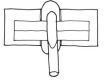

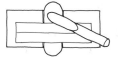

Note the large up-and-down handle movements that are not apparent in the normal view.

One final note about beads. Most people today think of a bead as simply an oval ridge on the surface of a cylinder, as shown at left in the photo on p. 109. In former times, however, turners always took the toe of a skew and incised a small groove, or "bevel," at each edge of the bead where it meets the cylinder (as shown at right in the photo on p. 109). On most furniture turnings this grooving entails only a light scribing cut with the toe of a skew, while on larger architectural turnings a definite groove is incised with repeated cuts of the skew.

Beveling the bead is a basic technique that adds tremendous impact to any turning by giving depth to the bead and setting it off from the surrounding spindle. On architectural turning, the bevel gives paint a place to flow, preventing a buildup of paint at the transition

Cutting a bead with a gouge

Begin with the gouge, flute up, at the center of the rondel (top left photo). Angle the tool to one side and roll it downhill, sliding it back slightly on the tool rest (above). Raise the tool handle and push forward as you approach the bottom of the bead (left). Return to the center of the bead and repeat the procedure on the other side (below).

A bead with narrow bevels at its base (right) has much greater visual impact than a bead without bevels (left).

point and a loss of visual impact. One reason that machine turnings look so lifeless is that they're made on cutterhead lathes that cannot cut bevels or undercuts. As a hand turner, you have a real advantage in creating shapes that can grab the eye of the viewer.

Turning square to round

One of the most frequent questions I'm asked in spindle-turning classes is, "How do I get from square to round without breaking out the corners?" The answer I always give is to use sharp tools and shear-cutting techniques. The actual mechanics of the cut depend on whether you want the transition from square to round to be a square shoulder or a concave or convex radius. Let's start with the square shoulder.

The best way to cut a square shoulder is to use the toe of a skew chisel. The tool must be held with the long corner down, its edge on the rest and the bevel at 90° to the work (see the drawing at right). This entails swinging the handle about 21°, which is half of the 42° inclusive grind angle . Use as much speed as is safe for the situation—in the 1,100-rpm to 1,700-rpm range for standard furniture turnings. Start by lightly scoring the work. Now move to the right (for a shoulder on the left) and widen the score mark. Go back and score the original mark deeper. Move to the right and remove the waste. This process is much like chopping a tree—the cut must always be wider than the inclusive

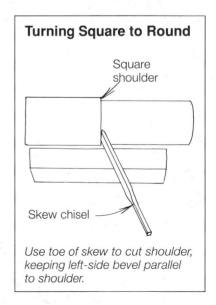

Turning Square to Round

Square shoulder

Skew chisel

Use toe of skew to cut shoulder, keeping left-side bevel parallel to shoulder.

grind angle of the chisel. Do this until the work is scored all the way around. You are left with a square shoulder on the left and a sloping cut on the right that meets up with the shoulder. Now use a spindle gouge to trim away the excess material up to the shoulder.

For this process to work, the tool should be level on the rest and touching at the exact centerline of the work. Only the very toe should touch. The tool's cutting edge must be absolutely vertical, because slanting it one way or the other will cause it to walk in that direction. Some care is necessary to use the tool with a light touch and to read the ghost so that the tool returns to the previous cut each time.

Often the transition from square to round is a concave or convex radius. Cutting the radius entails carefully reading the ghost, bringing a spindle gouge into a shear cut and rolling either a cove or a bead, depending on the shape desired. Again, running the lathe between 1,100 rpm and 1,700 rpm will help. Read the ghost, then bring the heel of the bevel in contact with the corners of the work. This is a highly interrupted cut and a light but firm touch works best. Trying to force the cut without the bevel rubbing will result in a catch and likely broken corners. Multiple passes are necessary, and restarting requires careful reading of the ghost.

Coping with harmonic chatter

An unwanted spiral pattern on thin spindle turnings is a problem that vexes all turners from time to time. Harmonic chatter, also called barber poling and rippling, occurs when spindle work becomes thin enough to flex along its length. As you touch a tool to the work it starts to vibrate between the centers of the lathe, much like the string of a musical instrument. The result is recurring flat spots that usually have a spiral pattern to them. At a minimum, the condition requires extra sanding, and at worst it ruins the work. Fortunately, there is much you can do to deal with harmonic chatter when you encounter it.

Since long, thin work is more prone to harmonic chatter than short, thick work, a logical progression of work when turning spindles can do much to prevent the condition. As much as possible, turn the thickest parts of a spindle first and the thinnest last. Work from the center of the spindle to the ends in a number of steps. For example, begin by turning the spindle to maximum diameter along its entire length. Next turn the center section. Then turn from the finished center portion to the thickest end, and complete the spindle by turning the thinnest end. Working in this progression leaves maximum support and rigidity in the spindle for the longest possible time. If you have to deal with chatter at all it will only be while you're turning the thinnest end.

If harmonic chatter is encountered, turning technique will do much to overcome the problem. Keeping the tool at 90° to the work rather than skewing it sideways helps, because in a sideways cut the tool bevel is rubbing on the area just previously cut. Any irregularity in this surface is immediately transmitted to the bevel and back to the work at the cutting edge, and the chatter gets worse and worse. If the tool is held at 90° to the work you deal only with the vibrating frequency of the work; you're not amplifying it.

A gouge overcomes harmonic chatter better than a skew, since a skew cuts a bit sideways even when the handle is square to the work (see pp. 86-87). By its very nature, a skew amplifies chatter. A spindle gouge overcomes chatter better than a roughing-out gouge because of its relatively narrower cutting edge.

Another very useful technique in overcoming harmonic chatter is to place the flesh of your palm against the work directly opposite the chisel, as shown in the photo below. Although this may sound dangerous, it's quite safe as long as the work is fully round. Use the thumb of your left hand to hold the tool on the rest and the palm of your hand to cradle the work. You needn't exert any great amount of pressure on

One way to overcome harmonic chatter on thin spindle turnings is to cradle the work in the palm of your left hand and hold the chisel on the rest with your thumb.

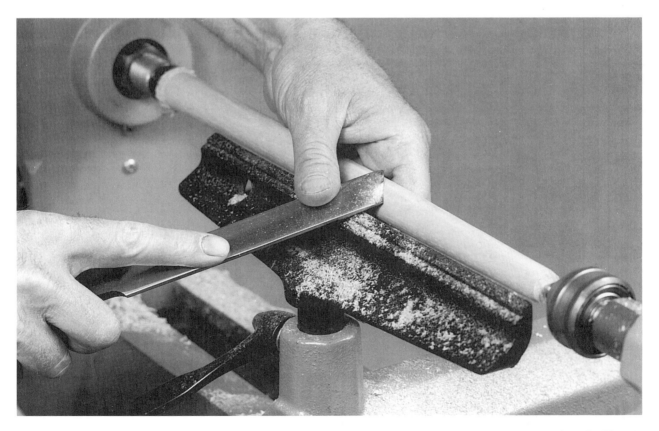

the work—if you're burning your flesh you're pushing too hard. Your hand acts merely to dampen the vibration, much as a guitarist fingers the string against a fret. The lower frequency caused by your dampening is usually enough to overcome harmonic chatter.

Steady rests

There comes a point where a spindle is so long and thin that the only way to prevent chatter is to use a steady rest to support the work. Many modern turners have great misconceptions about steady rests because they associate them with rests used in metalturning. In metalturning the tool is mounted on a carriage that rides along the bed ways of the machine, so the rest must support the work on exact center to avoid turning a taper. This requires surrounding the work with plane bearings or ball bearings for support. In woodturning the tool is guided by the turner, and exact centering by the steady rest is unimportant. Qualities needed in a woodturning steady rest are vibration dampening, support of the work to prevent it from bending away from the tool and quick adjustment.

As with chucks, I feel that the best steady rest is one that you make yourself. My plan for a steady rest, shown in the drawing on the facing page, follows closely one outlined by Frank Pain in his book *Practical Woodturner* (Sterling, 1990), which in turn is based on an early steady in the High Wycombe Museum, England. Except for the mention in Pain's book, the design has been largely forgotten, and today's commercial steadies trace their roots to metalturning.

The shopmade steady can be positioned at any point along the bed of the lathe and secured by a wood wedge. The metal beds on some lathes may make this mounting system impractical. In such instances a block under the bed ways with a carriage bolt and a nut to secure the steady is a good substitute. The movable tongue can be adjusted quickly to any size workpiece by raising and lowering the top wedge. If the wedge has a tendency to work loose, Pain suggests adding lead weight to the top of it. I have found that heavy rubber bands or strips of inner tube work better; they act as a spring and keep constant pressure on the tongue. Decreasing the taper also helps. To cut the 90° notch in the top wedge, simply mount a $\frac{1}{16}$-in. drill in the headstock (see pp. 136-137), set the steady on the bed and touch the movable tongue to the drill. Bandsaw a 90° corner at the drill mark, and the notch is at perfect center height for your lathe.

Shopmade Steady Rest

*Use available hardwood or good grade of plywood
(or combination of the two).*

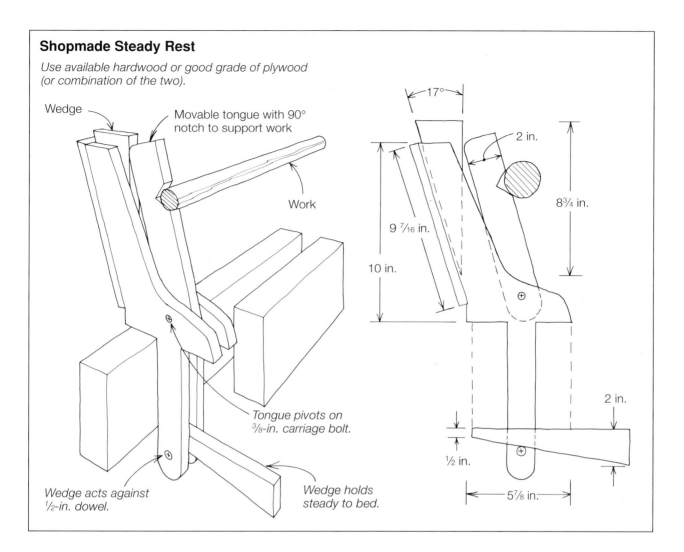

Wedge

Movable tongue with 90°
notch to support work

Work

Tongue pivots on
³⁄₈-in. carriage bolt.

Wedge acts against
¹⁄₂-in. dowel.

Wedge holds
steady to bed.

17°

2 in.

8³⁄₄ in.

9 ⁷⁄₁₆ in.

10 in.

2 in.

¹⁄₂ in.

5⁷⁄₈ in.

The advantage of this steady is that you can turn right through it, and it quickly readjusts to support the work at the new diameter. If you find that the workpiece becomes hot and starts to burn as it rubs against the sides of the notch, a little candle wax will provide the needed lubrication. Gluing a patch of nylon or Teflon to the notch area will also work.

In my experience, although all turners know that a steady rest is needed at times to overcome harmonic chatter, very few of them use one (I know of only two who do, besides myself). Most turners just live with the chatter and sand it out at the end. I believe that a steady rest is indispensable in spindle turning, whether you're making one part or many. The couple of hours spent making a steady will be repaid many times by better work, less sanding and less frustration.

If you encounter harmonic chatter in all your work no matter what corrective actions you take, the problem may be your lathe—specifically the bearings. If the bearings are worn to the point that there is excessive play you can expect almost constant harmonic chatter. For advice on replacing bearings, see pp. 142-148.

Duplication

Duplication seems to present a formidable problem to most turners. In fact, one of the most frequent questions I'm asked is, "What's the best duplicator to buy for my lathe?" My answer is always, "You're the best duplicator for your lathe." On the assumption that I'm joking (this is one of the few times I'm not), the turner in question finds a host of reasons why a duplicator is absolutely necessary. Over the years, I've concluded that duplicator dependence boils down to lack of confidence and a belief that "alike" means "identical," plus or minus one thousandth of an inch.

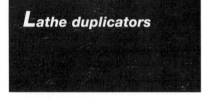

Lathe duplicators

While it's my firm belief that lathe duplicators have no place in the small shop, I concede that they can save a considerable amount of time on large-scale production jobs. A duplicator is an auxiliary carriage that's bolted onto a lathe bed with a knife connected to a pantograph that travels freely on the carriage. A master part is placed between centers in the duplicator, which is usually at the front of the lathe. A billet of the appropriate diameter is placed between the actual centers of the lathe. The pantograph then traces the master and moves the knife

Lathe duplicators can be timesavers for large-scale production work. (Photo by Charley Robinson.)

proportionally. Although some duplicators have sophisticated knives that cut tangentially, others make a simple scrape cut—the kind of cut I have been telling you to avoid.

If you're interested in learning more about lathe duplicators, I recommend you consult Charley Robinson's article on the subject in *Fine Woodworking* magazine, No. 86, pp. 68-73.

If you go into any antique store, calipers in hand, and take a close look at some pre-Machine-Age furniture, chances are that you'll be hard put to find any two turned parts that are exactly alike. Further study will invariably turn up some obvious discrepancies that you hadn't notice at first. The human eye has such a passion for symmetry that it will make things uniform even if they are not. This phenomenon is the stock in trade of the magician. Illusion capitalizes on the mind's desire to complete a task. Remove from your mind the impediment that any two turned pieces have to be *exactly* alike—they just have to be *nearly* alike.

Hand turning, when executed with first-class workmanship, yields turning detail that no machine can duplicate. Turning two or one hundred and two things alike is a basic skill that will develop as your turning skills improve. Like any other skill, using the correct procedures can help tremendously.

Establishing the major diameter

Any turning will have a maximum diameter at one or more points along its length. Since most turnings start from a square billet, this is usually the diameter that just brings it round. For example, with accurate centering on 2-in. stock, you will just turn round at about $1\frac{7}{8}$ in., give or take $\frac{1}{32}$ in. You don't need calipers to measure this—your roughing-out gouge (and your hands occasionally touching the spinning work) will tell you when things just come round. I generally turn the entire length of the piece to this major diameter. Once I've established the major diameter I use calipers to find other diameters.

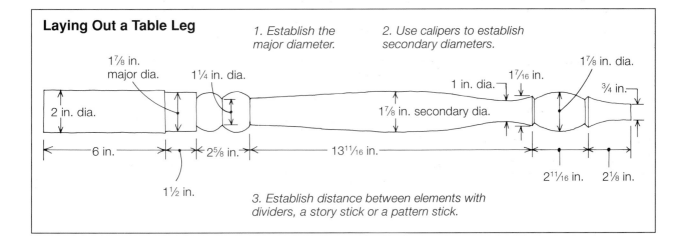

Laying Out a Table Leg

1. Establish the major diameter.

2. Use calipers to establish secondary diameters.

$1\frac{7}{8}$ in. major dia. $1\frac{1}{4}$ in. dia.

2 in. dia.

$1\frac{7}{8}$ in. secondary dia.

1 in. dia. $1\frac{7}{16}$ in.

$1\frac{7}{8}$ in. dia.

$\frac{3}{4}$ in.

6 in. $2\frac{5}{8}$ in. $13\frac{11}{16}$ in.

$1\frac{1}{2}$ in.

$2\frac{11}{16}$ in. $2\frac{1}{8}$ in.

3. Establish distance between elements with dividers, a story stick or a pattern stick.

Establishing secondary diameters

In addition to the major diameter, most turnings will have one or more readily apparent minor diameters. There are a number of ways to establish secondary diameters, using calipers, open-end wrenches or semaphores.

Calipers are a basic turning aid, and when you're duplicating parts you can never have enough of them. I comb flea markets for calipers, and regularly find top-quality calipers made by Starrett, Greenlee and Stanley for as little as $2.50 per pair. For a production run, I turn a master part and place it near my lathe so that it's available for visual reference. I then set a pair of calipers to each critical dimension. For small turnings I just set them out in order, usually on Palmer Sharpless's tool rack (see p. 27). For long turnings, I hang them by the turning at the place they measure (either on the wall, on a post by the lathe or on the steady rest).

If the design will allow it, I use the calipers in combination with a cut-off tool. While slicing into the work with the cutoff tool held in my right hand, I constantly monitor the progress with the calipers held in my left hand, as shown in the photo below. When the calipers just drop over the work I know I'm at the correct diameter. Some care

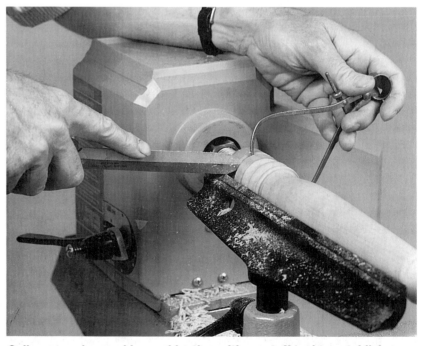

Calipers can be used in combination with a cutoff tool to establish a given diameter.

should be exercised here since it's possible for the calipers to bind in the slot you are chiseling in the work. If this happens they can go flying with dire results. For safety, always use a cutoff tool that's wider (by at least $\frac{1}{32}$ in.) than the calipers. Hold the calipers with a firm grip, but don't force them over the work—just allow them to drop over naturally. Finally, stand just to one side of the cut so that if the calipers do go flying you won't be in the line of fire. Where a cutoff tool cannot be used with the calipers, I just turn with the appropriate tool and use the calipers to monitor the diameter.

I also keep a set of inexpensive open-end wrenches hanging at the lathe for use as calipers to size tenons to specific drill sizes (they're also handy for lathe maintenance). Since an open-end wrench is slightly larger than an equivalent drill, you end up with a tenon that is a press fit. This trick, taught to me by my friend Leo Doyle, is a big timesaver because the wrenches are always set and ready for use. The wrench can be forced a bit at the last moment to compress the wood fibers of the tenon slightly. When water-based glue is applied the tenon swells, ensuring a lock-tight fit.

One other way to establish critical diameters is to use "semaphores." These are simply a series of adjustable toggles mounted on a beam behind the work. They rest on the work and drop over center when the desired diameter is reached. In my experience, semaphores would be useful only on a long-running, repeat job. In most instances, they take more time to set and adjust than it takes to do the actual turning.

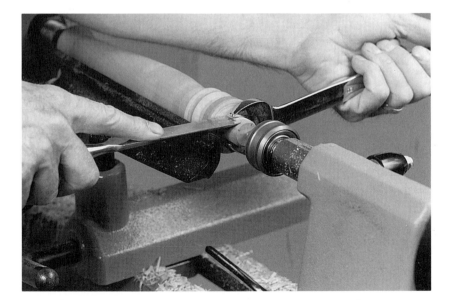

Use an open-end wrench to size tenons to diameter.

If you establish the major diameter by turning round and the minor diameter with calipers, everything else can be done by eye. The trick here is to play the same theme from piece to piece. If you use the same gouge to make each cove or bead (see p. 120), the contours will naturally come out close. The viewer's eye will pick up great discrepancies in the major and minor diameters but not much else. What the eye does pick up are discrepancies in the height of various elements on each turning. This problem can be overcome through the use of masking tape, dividers, story sticks and pattern sticks.

Spacing the elements

Placing everything at the right height along a spindle is the second important factor in maintaining the illusion of duplication. Starting with spindles that are all cut to exactly the same length will be a great help. For short spindles (ones that do not require the tool rest to be moved), taping a piece of masking tape across the tool rest is a direct technique that works well. Draw pencil lines on the tape at the critical points along the turning so that the elements can be placed quickly. (Beginners should transfer the marks from the tape to the spinning work.) I've found that tape works fine with one-time production runs of up to about fifteen pieces, but above that the tape wears out before you finish the job—not a good situation. Masking tape is not a good solution for repeat production jobs, because the tape leaves no record for the next run.

Dividers are useful for spacing the design elements along the spindle.

Similarly, dividers (which can also be found at bargain prices at flea markets) are handy for stepping off critical lengths along a spindle. By using several sets each element can be stepped off from the last. An additional advantage is that dividers both step off the distance and mark the spinning work. As with calipers, some care should be exercised when using dividers. Always rest both sides of the divider on the tool rest and do not overhang the tool rest too far (no more than $\frac{1}{4}$ in.). Never touch the dividers to anything but round work, and always use a light touch. Contacting square work can make two sharp divider points go flying. As with masking tape, the drawback to using dividers is that there is no stored record of the job.

For longer work and repetitive jobs, the best method of placing elements is with a story stick or a pattern stick. A story stick is made by cutting notches in a thin strip of wood ($\frac{1}{16}$ in. thick) that match the critical points in the turning. The notches can be cut with a backsaw, bandsaw or scrollsaw, or even a jackknife in a pinch. Once the work has been turned round the story stick is balanced on the tool rest. By placing a pencil or a scriber in each of the notches the information is transferred to the work.

A pattern stick is a good variation of the story stick, made by cutting a thin strip to the width of the billet you will start with, say 2 in. The spindle is then drawn out full scale on the face of the pattern stick, providing a visual reference of the relationship between the notches and the spindle and eliminating the need for a master part. Once you've laid out the critical diameters on the workpiece, simply place the pattern stick behind the part for visual reference.

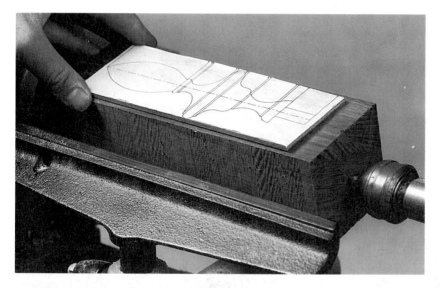

Make the pattern stick by cutting a thin strip of wood to the approximate width of the billet and drawing out the workpiece at full scale.

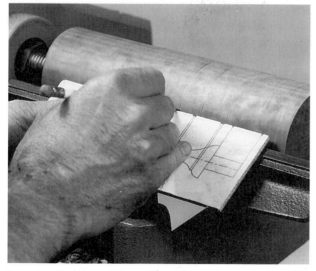

Transfer the layout lines from the pattern stick to the rounded billet.

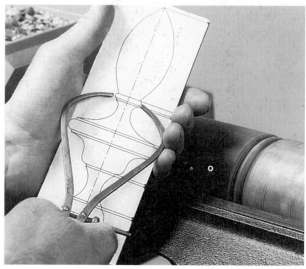

Use calipers to establish the secondary diameters.

The great advantage of using story and pattern sticks is that, unlike masking tape and dividers, they provide a stored record of the spindle profile for jobs that are run repeatedly. Once you've finished duplicating a set of spindles, file away the stick (and a sample part) in a drawer or hang it on a nail in the workshop. You'll be glad you have a pattern to work from when the time comes to run the job again.

Using the right tool for the job

Tools, especially gouges, are a great help in duplication. Each gouge will optimally cut a particular sweep of cove or bead. I treasure a very old set of four Buck Brothers gouges that were made around 1915 (shown in the photo at left). If I use the appropriate size gouge, depending on the sweep of the cove or bead I'm turning, it's an easy matter to achieve the same theme. The moral: Match the tool to the job.

There are, of course, instances where only a scraper can get the job done, and special-ground scrapers can be a great aid in achieving and duplicating a unique shape. In metalworking, a tool that has its face ground to conform to the desired shape is called a "form tool." To make your own form tool, grind the top of an old file smooth. Now draw the desired shape out to scale on paper. Glue the paper to the top of the freshly ground surface, then grind the bevel of the tool to the drawn shape. Be sure to grind 15° to 20° of clearance in the bevel.

Special-ground scrapers are also available commercially. Sorby sells scrapers in three sizes for the purpose of turning "captive rings," which are rings trapped on a spindle that, to the uninitiated, appear to defy logic. The photo essay on p. 122 unlocks the mystery of captive rings.

Looking at two places at once

One final aid in duplication is what I call "seeing the big picture." When you first start turning you tend to concentrate on the point where the tool is touching the work and little else. As you gain confidence, you should be able simultaneously to see the outline of the spindle. By looking tangentially at the top edge of the work, you'll see its shape clearly, just as if you were looking at a mechanical drawing of that half of the spindle. For some people, throwing their eyes slightly out of focus helps in this process. This is also part of reading the ghost, or seeing the outline of the billet when it is not yet square.

Matching the gouge to the profile of the cove or bead can be a great aid in duplication.

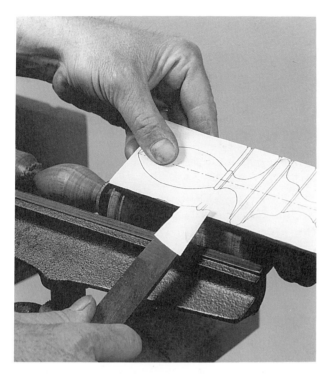

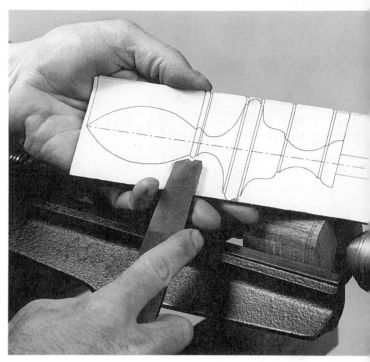

Grinding an old file to match
the profile of a small detail will
enable you to achieve and
duplicate unique shapes.

Making captive rings using Sorby form tools

To cut a captive ring, begin by raising a bead with the center scraper (above). Switch to the right-hand scraper and undercut the bead (above right). Then use the left-hand scraper to free the ring from the spindle (right). Now watch your friends try to figure out how you got the ring on the spindle (below right). For a photo of the finished captive ring, see the photo essay on French polishing on p. 127.

Sanding

While one of the main purposes of this book is to teach methods that eliminate excessive sanding, there comes a point in most turnings where some sanding is necessary. If you use the shear-cutting methods I've recommended, you should be able to start sanding for spindle turning at 150 or 180 grit rather than 60 or 80 grit, which would be the case if you were scrape-cutting. Sanding face work (in most woods) starts at a heavier grit—usually 60 or 80 grit.

Sanding spindle work

The work remains in the lathe for sanding. For beginners, it makes sense to remove the tool rest. Experienced turners work around the rest by sanding at the back of the piece, as shown in the photo below, left. Never use a whole (or even a large) sheet of sandpaper since it can wrap around the spindle and drag your fingers in with dire results. I always tear sandpaper into quarter sheets, then fold these in half. For spindle turnings, I generally start with 180 grit and finish with 220 grit, although you can go as fine as you like. The main thing is not to skip grades of sandpaper or you'll get scratch marks on the work. With good spindle techniques, sanding is merely a final operation to remove fuzz and make things uniform in texture for finish. Once you've finished sanding, its a good idea to burnish a turning with a handful of chips to improve surface finish (shown below right).

To sand without removing the tool rest, hold the sandpaper at the back of the spinning workpiece.

Burnish the spindle with a handful of shavings to improve surface finish.

Sanding face work

Face work takes a good deal of sanding even with textbook turning techniques. An experienced turner will spend as much time sanding face work as turning it. Start with 60-grit or 80-grit sandpaper to remove the tearout in the end grain, then work up through grades to the desired finish. A common sanding schedule might run 60, 100, 150, 220 and so on. If providence allows you to start at 80 grit, then the schedule might run 120, 180, 220.

Although hand sanding works fine for spindle work, the best way to sand face work is with a flexible pad mounted in an electric drill (see p. 180). The rubber pad is flexible enough for most face work. There are various proprietary systems available. One uses hook-and-loop fasteners (Velcro®) to attach the sanding media to the disc. Another system uses sanding circles that are backed with pressure-sensitive adhesive. A third system has a metal or plastic clutch glued to the back of the sanding circle. All three systems allow quick changing of abrasive to work up through finer grades. With the Velcro® and clutch systems, coarser grades can be reused if they're not expended, but I use pressure-sensitive adhesive disks, which are usually cheaper than the other systems on a per-sheet basis.

Holding the spinning disc against the spinning work makes sanding go much faster than if you were sanding by hand. Since the disc wipes at an angle to the direction that the piece was turned, a smoother surface is achieved. The important thing to remember when power sanding is to spend enough time at the coarser grits to remove all of the tearout.

These sanding systems are unsuitable for sanding beyond 180 grit, because at finer grits there will be circular scratches even though the surface becomes more polished generally. The reason is that dirt and oversize sanding particles occasionally counteract the action of the majority of the sanding particles in the paper. The solution is to glue foam rubber (I use ⅜-in. neoprene rubber) to an expended pad, then glue thin flexible sandpaper to the foam. The resilience of the foam combined with the flexibility of the thin paper allows you to sand ultra-fine grades with ease. A thin piece of garnet sandpaper glued to the foam rubber with photo-mount adhesive works splendidly. When the sandpaper needs changing, a few blasts from a hair dryer will loosen the glue joint so the sandpaper can be removed.

Finishing

Just as the lathe can be a great aid in reducing the drudgery of sanding, it can also help in the finishing process. In most cases, turned furniture parts will be finished with whatever is planned for the rest of the piece, and a considerable amount of time can be saved by finishing them right after they've been turned rather than when the piece is assembled. As outlined in Chapter 2, it's a good idea to reference the turned piece to the drive center with a mark. This mark allows you to rechuck the piece with each of the center tines in the same place and maintain centering. For example, if you wanted twelve spindles, you would turn them all first, then rechuck and stain, and finally resand and finish.

Stains and most finishes can be wiped on with a small rag while the lathe is running at a low speed. I use a rag about 2 in. square, which is small enough that it won't pull your fingers in with it should it get

Correcting mistakes

Everybody, even the experienced turner, makes a mistake at the lathe now and then. Although it's tempting just to throw the work in the corner and start again, there are a number of ways to sweep the blemish under the rug, so to speak. For example, a cove can be widened and/or deepened slightly, and beads can be cut to a lower profile. You're probably the only one who will ever know about such subtle changes. If you break a piece off a bead, it can be glued back on (assuming, of course, that you can find it amongst the shavings under your lathe). If you can't find the chip, you can always plane the spot flat, glue a new piece on and re-turn the work. A chipped corner or bead

can often be turned to the inside of the finished piece of furniture during assembly. Just think of it as "antiquing."

A handy glue to use for repairs is cyanoacrylate ("super") glue. To fix a small blemish caused by a catch, fill the area with glue and sprinkle some shavings into the glue. On some woods this can be a very convincing fix. Cyanoacrylate glue is also good for arresting checks at the end of a workpiece and for gluing small objects to a glue block (it's what I used to hold the tagua nut on the glue block in the photo essay on pp. 134-135).

Cyanoacrylate glue is available from woodworking suppliers and model shops in three viscosities: water thin, medium (my preferred grade) and thick. A catalyst is also sold that will speed up setting time to about 20 to 30 seconds. Take care when

working with this glue, since it will glue skin instantly. Avoid the temptation to hold the work with your fingers while the glue sets, or you may end up glued to the work. Cyanoacrylate glue is also very irritating to the eyes, so always wear safety glasses and work with plenty of ventilation.

For architectural turnings that are going to be painted, holes can be patched with auto-body putty (Bondo is a common brand). This material can even be used to replace broken beads: patch the break with a blob of the putty and then re-turn.

Stick shellac works wonders for small blemishes. Use a black stick shellac on cherry and it will look just like a pitch pocket. Remember there are no mistakes, just new design opportunities.

caught in the spinning work—an important safety consideration. I often burnish an oil finish with shavings, usually about five minutes after applying the finish. Since burnishing with shavings wipes across the grain, there is good filling of pores.

One finish that's easy to apply with the workpiece in the lathe merits special mention here. This is a lathe-applied French polish, which gives all the beauty of the traditional method but takes much less time and bother. To French-polish turner-style you need to use genuine orange shellac made from shellac flakes. The canned variety has preservatives and extenders to prolong shelf life, which render it unsuitable for French polish. I prefer to make my own shellac from pure grain alcohol, which I obtain from my local druggist (in a pinch I've used 200-proof grain alcohol sold in liquor stores as Ever Clear).

I mix my shellac in 200ml plastic camping bottles, filling the bottle about a quarter full of shellac flakes and adding alcohol to just shy of the top. I shake the bottle well, and again every hour or so until everything dissolves, then set it in direct sunlight for at least a day. The wax and impurities settle out. I decant the liquid, which is pure orange shellac, and throw away the sediment.

To French-polish in the lathe, apply a coat of the shellac mixture to the work with a small rag or a full brush (which can be cleaned with a mixture of ammonia and water), as shown in the top photo on the facing page. However you apply the shellac, the important point is to saturate the work completely—don't worry if some of it dribbles onto the lathe bed. Remove the tool rest, stand aside and start the lathe. You need plenty of speed here—at least 1,700 rpm. Grab a handful of shavings and apply them with firm pressure to the spinning work, as shown in the middle photo on the facing page. Turn the shavings often since they will become saturated with the excess shellac. The shellac will melt under the burnishing action of the shavings, leaving a pleasing French polish with none of the fuss, pumice, oil and other assorted trappings of conventional French polishing.

French polish is a very thin finish, yet it is quite durable, except to water, which will leave a white mark. To give the finish some water resistance and further beauty, I apply pure carnauba wax to the spinning work. Pure carnauba, which is difficult to find, is very hard and shatters like ice if dropped. Crayon the wax onto the work (shown in the bottom left photo on the facing page) and finish by burnishing with shavings again.

French polishing

Apply the shellac to the work with a small rag (shown at left). Then burnish the spinning work with a handful of shavings (center). To improve the finish, hold carnauba wax to the spinning work (below left), then burnish again for a durable, beautiful finish (below right).

Advanced turning techniques

Now that we've looked at the basic turning techniques and learned how to duplicate a spindle turning and sand and finish it to completion, it's time to explore some more advanced turning techniques that you may be interested in trying as your turning skills develop. These techniques include paper joints, offset turning, cutting flutes and reeds, chatter work and turning materials other than wood.

Paper joints

Using paper joints to chuck work in the lathe was described in Chapter 2 (see p. 58), and the same principle can be used to turn furniture parts. The most common application for paper joints is to make split turnings, which are identical turned halves used as an embellishment on a piece of furniture. A simple split column is shown in the photo essay on the facing page.

To produce a split turning, the two halves of the workpiece are glued together before turning, with a piece of brown kraft paper (I use a grocery bag) inserted in the glue joint. As with any glue joint, a joinery-level fit is necessary, so hand-plane or joint the pieces to achieve a perfect match. Use hide glue for the best paper joint.

For a perfect split turning, center the workpiece in the lathe exactly on the parting line. This is one application where it's best to use a ring tailstock center rather than a 60° point because the latter might split the joint. Turning a piece such as the column shown in the photo essay is straightforward spindle turning. After turning, unchuck the piece and insert a sharp chisel into the joint. A sharp rap with a mallet will cleave the joint down the center and produce two identical halves.

Paper joints can also be used in faceplate work, as for the pair of drawer fronts for a Queen Anne desk shown in the photos on the facing page. The drawer fronts are each one-half of a split turning and chucked by a paper joint. Glue the paper-jointed drawer blanks to a glue block, making sure that the joint is on the centerline of the glue block. Then mount the drawer fronts in the headstock and faceplate-turn. Separate the finished drawer fronts from the glue block and from each other with a chisel.

Paper-jointing a column and drawer fronts

Glue up the blanks for the split column with brown kraft paper in the joint (shown at right). After spindle-turning the column, use a sharp chisel to separate the halves (below left). Glue the blanks for the drawer fronts along the centerline of the glue block, paper-jointing the top edges of the drawer fronts (center right). The turned drawer fronts, still glued together, can be seen in the photo below. The bead around the perimeter of the drawer front (bottom left) was scraped with a form tool. The photo at bottom right shows the finished drawer fronts (with the glue block they were turned on) and the split column.

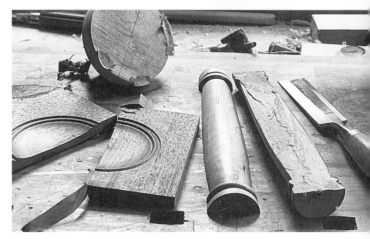

Offset turning

Offset turning is accomplished by turning between centers at two different locations on the end of a spindle. The most common use of offset turning is in the making of cabriole legs for furniture. I have used it other times to make such items as the shaving-brush stand shown in the photo at left. I turned the stand much like a crankshaft. I first turned a 2½-in. cylinder, then offset the cylinder at a point about ¼ in. from the edge but with the center points in the same axis. I now turned the connecting column, and then cut the C-shaped openings for the base and brush with a jeweler's hacksaw.

It's not possible to make a true cabriole leg by turning, only the effect is achieved. Still, turned cabriole legs were often made, even in the 18th century. Sometimes sculpted cabriole legs were installed on the front of a Queen Anne piece and turned legs were placed at the back, probably to save money. The technique was used on Queen Anne chairs, stools and small tables. Turned legs could be found on Country Queen Anne pieces of all types, presumably because the technique was cheaper and less demanding.

Cabriole legs can be turned in two ways—using converging axes or parallel axes. In the former, both ends of the leg are offset, but toward an opposite corner so that the two axes converge just below the pommel. In the latter, both ends are offset, but with the centers on the

This shaving-brush stand was made by turning a cylinder between offset centers.

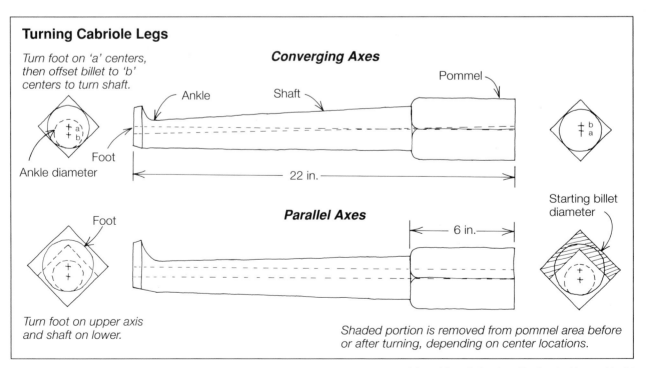

Adapted from *Queen Anne Furniture* by Norman Vandal

same axis. Parallel axes are the easier to turn, and the best-known example of this type of turning is the Dutch-influenced "duck-footed" chairs made in the Hudson River Valley from about 1750 to 1810.

For parallel axes, you need to begin with a larger starting billet. Depending on where the centers fall, the pommel area is reduced to the desired size after layout or after turning. The foot is first turned to the desired diameter on the parallel offsets. The billet is then rechucked on the pommel centers for turning the shaft and ankle. Parallel-axes legs have a vertical shaft, whereas legs with converging axes have a shaft that slopes inward from the offset corner. If you're interested in turning cabriole legs, you should consult Norman Vandal's book *Queen Anne Furniture* (The Taunton Press, 1990), which has an extensive description of the technique. I also recommend *Woodturning for Cabinetmakers* (Sterling, 1990) by Michael Dunbar, which has a chapter on offset turning.

Cutting flutes and reeds

Architecture and period furniture often have turnings with decorative elements such as flutes and reeds. Flutes and reeds can be thought of as coves and beads that run along the length of a spindle turning rather than around it. Flutes are concave grooves cut in the surface of the work, whereas reeds are convex beads raised on the surface.

Because flutes and reeds run along the axis of the work, they can't be turned, but they can be made in the lathe while the machine is not running. This type of work can be accomplished by employing a router in a jig in conjunction with the lathe's indexing mechanism. There are many jigs for cutting flutes and reeds. One of the best designs I have seen was one submitted to *Fine Woodworking* magazine (issue No. 38) by Dennis Preston of Brookfield, Connecticut (see the top drawing on p. 132). Preston's jig is basically a right-angle plate that positions a router on the lathe centerline. It has a couple of advantages over jigs that work from above: first, the cut can be easily monitored (most other jigs work blind), and, second, the standoff around the bit controls the depth of cut, making the bit follow the contour of the turning (most other jigs will cut only straight tapers and then only with a good deal of finagling).

While flutes can easily be cut with a core-box bit, reeds are not as simple to make. The best setup is to use a special router bit in conjunction with the jig shown in the bottom drawing on p. 132. This is a variation of Dennis Preston's jig with the router axis turned 90°. It was submitted to *Fine Woodworking* magazine (issue No. 39) by James B. Small of Shippensburg, Pennsylvania. When setting up a jig for fluting or reeding, always make some trial cuts on a test piece first. And when

Dennis Preston's Fluting Jig

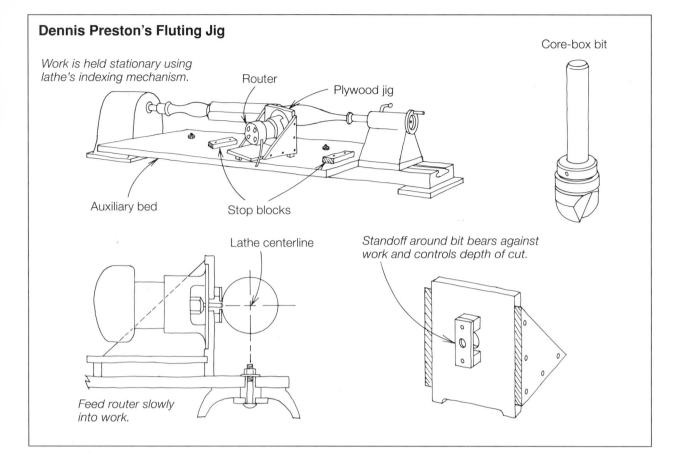

Work is held stationary using lathe's indexing mechanism.

Router

Plywood jig

Core-box bit

Auxiliary bed

Stop blocks

Lathe centerline

Standoff around bit bears against work and controls depth of cut.

Feed router slowly into work.

James Small's Reeding Jig

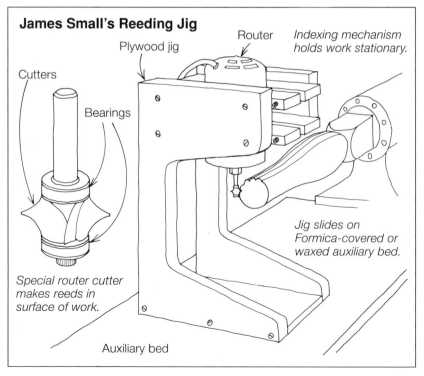

Plywood jig

Router

Indexing mechanism holds work stationary.

Cutters

Bearings

Jig slides on Formica-covered or waxed auxiliary bed.

Special router cutter makes reeds in surface of work.

Auxiliary bed

using core-box bits, make several passes at increasing depths rather than a single pass at the desired finish depth. Shallower cuts will make the router easier to control and improve the surface finish of the work.

There are a number of ways to lay out the flutes and reeds on the turning. The standard method is to use the lathe's indexing mechanism, which allows you to lock the spindle at equal intervals around the circumference of the work (see pp. 15-16). If your lathe lacks an index head, you can use one of the after-market chucks that offers indexing. Another alternative is to screw a disc of plywood to a faceplate. Leave a hole at the center of the disc, so that a spur center may be used in the normal way. Lay out the desired number of holes around the perimeter of the disc. A radius will divide a circle into six parts, so equal hole spacing is easy with a pair of dividers or a compass. All that is necessary now is to use a pin to engage the holes and lock the spindle.

Chatter work

Earlier I told you what steps to take to avoid chatter in your work (see the discussion of harmonic chatter on pp. 110-111). Now I'm going to explain how you can deliberately use chatter as a design element. In this sense, chatter is a decorative pattern cut in the end grain. Chatter work has been practiced for centuries, especially in the Far East. I often see small Japanese and Chinese turned items (c. 1970 and earlier) at antique shops and flea markets with splendid chatter work.

Chatter-work decoration is cut in the end grain of hard woods using a specially ground scraper. This lidded box is the piece that was turned in the photo essay on jam-chucking (see pp. 52-53).

The principle of chatter work is simplicity itself. A scraper of the appropriate shape is ground from a thin strip of spring steel. The strip is sufficiently thin that it will vibrate when presented to the work in a downhill scrape cut. It is this vibration that creates the decorative pattern.

Chatter work can only be cut in the end grain of reasonably hard woods or other hard materials such as ivory nut (tagua) and plastic. The thickness of the spring steel and how far out it is extended unsupported affect the frequency of vibration and the appearance of the chatter work. The chatter pattern is also affected by the angle at which the tool is presented. Holding the tool on the centerline of the work will produce a linear pattern; presenting above center will make a counterclockwise spiral, and below center, a clockwise spiral. Experiment on test pieces to see which pattern you prefer. For best results, use the chatter work in small amounts and set it off in bands with grooves or raised areas in between.

The edge of the chatter tool needs to be a very small round nose or a V-shape no more than about ¼ in. wide. I've often demonstrated chatter work by grinding a chunk of old sawblade to the desired profile and holding it in vise grips. A dedicated chatter tool designed by Oregon turner Dennis Stewart is available from Sorby (see the Sources

of Supply on pp. 191-192). It has a spring-steel cutter ground to a V, which can be easily moved back and forth in the handle to change the resonating frequency (see the photo at left).

Turning other materials

Most substances that can be worked with hand tools can also be turned. One day after lunch, in a fit of euphoria, I even turned two carrots and a zucchini. Materials that are more commonly turned include bone, ivory, amber, horn, shells, plastic, soapstone and ivory nut, which is the nut of the ivory palm tree. All of these substances

Sorby makes a dedicated chatter tool with a spring-steel cutter ground to a V.

Turning a knob from ivory nut

Ivory nuts make ideal knobs for cabinets and drawers. Chuck the nut on a glue block in the headstock (shown below left). Use a spindle gouge to turn the knob (below right and bottom left), raising a small nub on its face (bottom right). Sand and burnish the knob (top left and right, facing page), then use a parting tool to separate it from the glue block (bottom left and right, facing page).

take well to shear-cutting techniques, except for stone, which must be scraped. Alabaster is fun to turn and the results are beautiful, but be sure to do it when you can open a window, or better yet, take the lathe outside since the dust will cloud up the entire shop. I often turn knobs from ivory nut. The best way to chuck such items is to glue them to a glue block.

All of the materials mentioned in the previous paragraph take well to buffing. I use a small buffing wheel mounted on an arbor in an electric drill and buff the work while it's spinning in the lathe. Stainless-steel compound works well and doesn't show on most materials. The results are a mirror-like finish. For more on buffing, see the discussion on pp. 75-77.

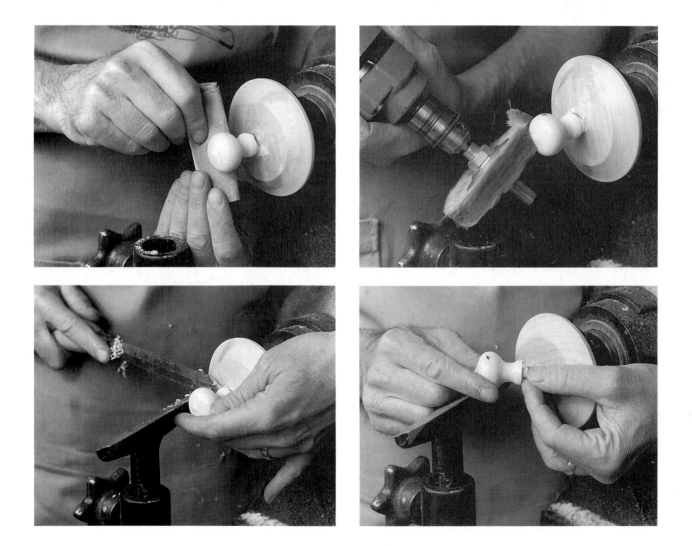

Drilling in the lathe

One of the ancillary uses of the lathe that's often overlooked is drilling. For many years, I survived quite well using a lathe as a drill press, and there is no reason that you cannot do the same for most general woodworking applications. Drilling in the lathe can be accomplished with the drill mounted in the headstock or the tailstock (which is another good reason to buy a lathe with Morse tapers in both spindles). The normal accessory used to hold drills is a drill chuck, or Jacobs chuck (see p. 49). Unless otherwise stated, for the rest of this section it should be assumed that the drill is held in a chuck.

Before discussing the various ways to drill in the lathe, I'd first like to clarify the distinction between drilling and boring. To a metalworker, drilling in a lathe is using a drill of any type to make a hole in the workpiece. Boring is using a tool to turn an existing hole larger. The advantage of boring over drilling is that the wall of the hole is perfectly concentric with the axis of the lathe. To a woodworker, drilling and boring are interchangeable terms, and I will hold with that convention in the discussion that follows.

Drilling in the tailstock

The commonest way to drill in the lathe is with the drill chuck mounted in the tailstock. The work is held on a faceplate or in a chuck, and the appropriate drill is held in the tailstock. The lathe is started at the appropriate speed for the drill, and the drill is slowly advanced into the spinning work. It's a simple and straightforward operation, but there are some fine points that can make for better work.

First, it's important that the drill point start on the exact center of the work. Two things can help here. One is to face the work level with a scraper or a gouge before drilling starts—an uneven work face will make the drill work unevenly as it just touches the work, causing it to veer off center. Another aid to centering is to cut a small dimple at the exact center for the drill point to start in. This can be done easily with a ¼-in. spindle gouge or a V-tipped scraper.

Second, it's important to clear the drill with sufficient frequency. As the hole deepens, the flutes of the drill can become impacted with chips, and the drill will bind and/or burn. I've seen drills buried so tightly that the work had to be split with a chisel to free them. To clear the chips from the flutes, back the drill almost all the way out of the hole and allow the chips to fall away. The deeper a drill bores, the more often it has to be cleared. While at first you may be able to drill

Most drills can be mounted in a drill chuck for drilling in the lathe, with the exception of the spade bit shown at left, which should be avoided.

$\frac{1}{8}$ in. or even $\frac{1}{4}$ in. without clearing, as the job progresses clearing will be required every $\frac{1}{16}$ in. or less. As a rule, smaller drills require more frequent clearing than larger ones.

Drilling in the headstock

A great many drilling tasks can also be accomplished with the drill mounted in the headstock. In this configuration, the lathe works much like a drill press, albeit horizontally rather than vertically. This method is particularly good for drilling holes in spindle turnings when the hole needs to be both concentric and aligned with the axis of the piece. A good example is drilling tool handles (see the photo on p. 138).

To drill with the headstock, the original center mark on the work is placed against the point of the spinning drill. The work is caught on the opposite end by the tailstock center. You have to hold the work with your left hand to keep it from spinning, while turning the tailstock handwheel to advance the work into the drill. Since you are dependent on the strength of your left hand to keep the work from spinning, this operation is only suitable for relatively small drill sizes ($\frac{1}{2}$ in. or less). It is possible for the drill to veer off center and break out the side of the work, which is why you should always hold the work well ahead of the desired depth so that if breakthrough occurs you will not drill into your hand. For added safety, run the lathe at moderate to low speed (1,100 rpm or less) when drilling in the headstock.

If you really want to make your lathe into a drill press, you can fit a drill pad—in effect, a mini drill-press table—into the tailstock spindle. Years ago, drill pads were a common accessory for both metal and wood lathes, but now you'll probably have to make your own since they're

Tool handles can be drilled with the drill mounted in the headstock. Hold the handle with your left hand to prevent it from spinning as you advance the work into the drill by turning the tailstock handwheel.

hard to find. The drawing below shows a plan for a drill pad that will fit a #2 Morse-taper spindle. For strength, the pad is best made in two pieces, using a hardwood such as maple or red oak. The Morse taper is spindle-turned, while the pad is faceplate-turned.

In use, a drill of the appropriate diameter is placed in the headstock and the work is placed on the drill pad (see the top photos on the facing page). The tailstock handwheel is then used to advance the table and work into the drill. As in drilling with a drill press, make sure you can hold the work with sufficient leverage to keep it from spinning. The bigger the drill, the more leverage you'll require.

Drill Pad

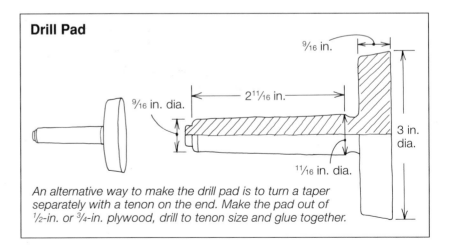

9/16 in.

9/16 in. dia.

2¹¹/16 in.

3 in. dia.

¹¹/16 in. dia.

An alternative way to make the drill pad is to turn a taper separately with a tenon on the end. Make the pad out of ¹/₂-in. or ³/₄-in. plywood, drill to tenon size and glue together.

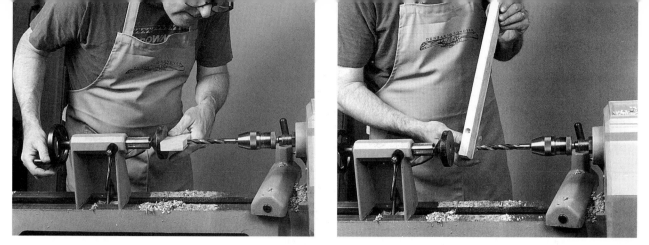

Using a drill pad in the tailstock provides support for the work as you drill in the headstock.

Drilling with pod augers

Another way to drill small-diameter holes through the axis of a spindle turning is to use a hand-held pod auger, or lamp auger, which looks much like a spoon bit with a long handle attached. Used correctly, pod augers are easier to keep on center than other types of drills.

Pod augers can be used in two ways, depending on the design of your lathe. If the lathe has a hollow tailstock spindle, the work can be mounted on a special tailstock cup center that has its point removed. The pod auger is then inserted into the spinning work through the back of the tailstock spindle. If your lathe doesn't have a hollow tailstock spindle, you'll have to buy a special fixture (available from specialty turning suppliers) to drill with a pod auger through the tailstock.

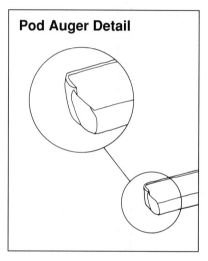

Pod Auger Detail

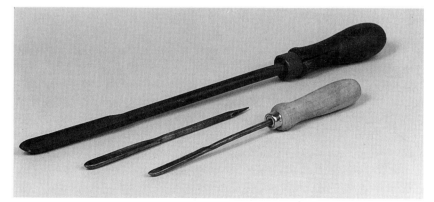

Pod augers can be used through the tailstock to drill small-diameter holes through the center of a spindle turning.

CHAPTER 5

Maintenance, Repair and Modification

When you buy a new car you spend the first few thousand miles "breaking it in," and the rest of its life "wearing it out." So it is with a lathe. Maintenance is required on a regular basis, and sooner or later repair is necessary. Maintenance and repair are tasks that most of us tend to neglect for one reason or another. My sense is that most people aren't quite sure what to do. In this chapter, I'll explain what must be done to keep your lathe running in tip-top condition and suggest some things that may make it run even better.

This chapter is also intended as an aid to buying a used lathe. A machine with a few years under its V, poly-V or flat belt often represents an exceptional value and may possess features you would have to pay a lot for in a new machine. My father and I have purchased many classic woodturning lathes at bargain prices, and all have more than lived up to our expectations. As my father aptly sums it up, "In former times honest construction was the rule, and manufacturers weren't afraid to pour a little metal in the mold." Like the Rolls Royce salesman, I like to think of classic machines not as used, but as previously owned. A little love and maintenance will restore such machines to their original condition.

Worn bearings must be replaced to keep the lathe running in prime condition. Bearing replacement requires disassembly of the headstock.

Replacing bearings

In the unlikely event that you have an old lathe with plain bearings, you can keep the lathe running smoothly by oiling the bearings on a daily basis. Most lathes today, even those found on the used market, are equipped with ball bearings that are lubricated and "sealed for life" (see the photo on p. 14). These bearings don't require any regular maintenance, but they do need to be replaced every few years.

The sides of the ball bearing are sealed with plastic, which retains the grease packed into the bearing during assembly. Age and use take their toll on any grease, even in a sealed-for-life bearing. Eventually, the grease fails and the bearing fails shortly thereafter. I've always joked that a "sealed for life" bearing is just that: It's sealed for *its* life, which is however long it takes for the grease to fail. Fortunately, this is usually a good long time.

If you use your lathe on a regular basis, you probably won't notice the gradual loss of bearing performance. If your bearings are more than five years old, however, chances are they're anemic, if not spent, and it's time to think about replacing them. A good test for worn bearings is to remove tension from the belt, which leaves the headstock spindle free to turn without resistance. Spin the spindle by placing your hand on the pulley. If the spindle spins freely and the bearings have a "dry" sound and feel, the grease is dry. (If the grease is still good, the spindle will have a slightly dead feel and not want to spin freely.) The first order of business is to remove the offending bearings.

I can't offer a definite prescription for removing bearings since no two headstock designs are the same. However, understanding how a typical bearing assembly goes together should help you figure out any headstock. The surfaces of the bearings and the bearing seats (the areas on the spindle where the bearings ride and the pockets in the headstock that hold them) are machined to strict tolerances. There are two types of fit for the bearing seats: a sliding fit and a press fit. In a sliding fit, the two mating surfaces can slide over each other but there is no radial play. In a press fit, a slightly larger diameter is pressed into a slightly smaller mating diameter. Such assemblies require an arbor press to put them together (see the photo at left).

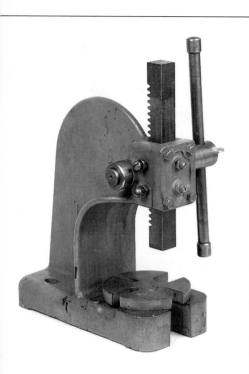

An arbor press can exert tremendous, but perfectly axial, force on shaft assemblies. While older presses were mechanical, newer ones are generally hydraulic.

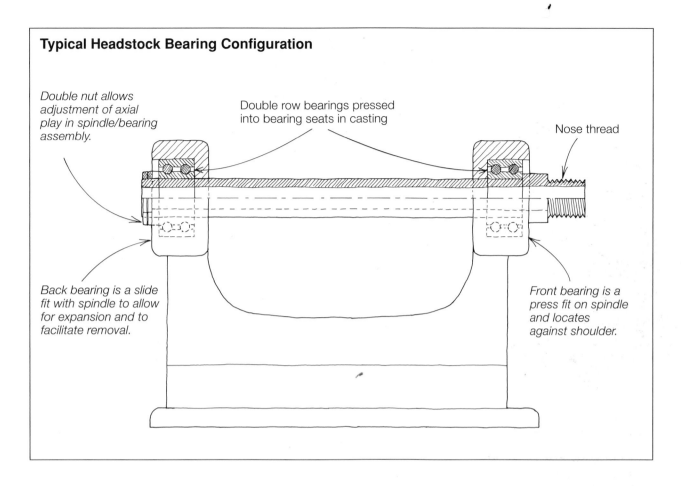

Typical Headstock Bearing Configuration

Double nut allows adjustment of axial play in spindle/bearing assembly.

Double row bearings pressed into bearing seats in casting

Nose thread

Back bearing is a slide fit with spindle to allow for expansion and to facilitate removal.

Front bearing is a press fit on spindle and locates against shoulder.

Because the headstock spindle expands as it heats up during use, at least one of the bearing seats must be a slide fit. A common configuration is shown in the drawing above. The bearings are a press fit into the headstock casting. The front bearing is a press fit against the shoulder on the spindle. (The other side of this shoulder is the shoulder for the nose thread.) The back bearing is a slide fit with the spindle.

Most lathes have additional fittings to hold and cover the bearings. Often, metal rings screw into place with three or more screws around the spindle, and these may contain seals that further protect the bearing. A common design is to have a fine thread on the back of the spindle (the end opposite the nose) on which there are two nuts. The first nut is run up against the inner race of the bearing and adjusted until there is no play in the assembly. The second nut is then locked against the first. Sometimes a wavy washer is interposed between the nuts and the bearing as well, its purpose being to remove play from the assembly. This washer should be replaced with the bearings because it invariably takes a set. Snap rings are used extensively today, and there are usually an array of spacers and washers involved. As you disassemble the headstock, make a careful note of the order in which all of these parts are taken off so that everything can be reassembled in perfect order.

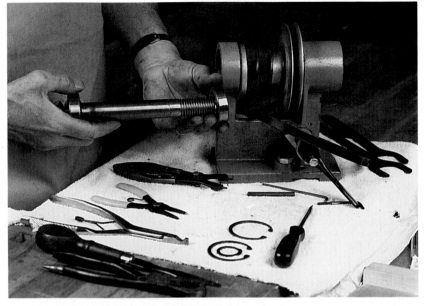

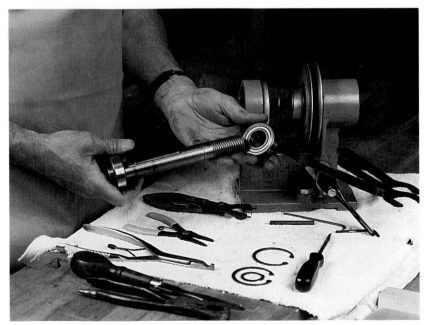

Disassembly of the headstock (here the Delta 46-700) requires the removal of various fittings, including the snap ring that retains the rear bearing (shown above). Once the headstock is disassembled, the slide-fit bearing (in this case the front bearing) can be removed. The rear bearing will be removed with an arbor press.

Bearing pullers are used to remove the bearings from the headstock spindle. The puller at right is for removing small bearings from shaft assemblies, while the larger model at left can adjust to a variety of situations.

Once you've taken the headstock apart, there are a variety of ways to remove the bearings from the spindle. One method is to use a bearing puller (see the photo above). A tool of this type would be used for removing the back bearing, and possibly the front, from our typical headstock in the drawing on p. 143. To remove a press-fit bearing from the spindle, you'll usually need an arbor press. Often the entire headstock must be placed in a press. You can sometimes improvise an arbor press using the bench dogs of a European-style workbench (see the sidebar on p. 146).

Although it's tempting to pound the assembly apart using soft-faced mallets and blocks of wood, I strongly urge you not to do this since this practice can ruin the bearings by putting flat spots on the balls. While it makes no difference in the disassembly, it does in the assembly. Since one is merely the reverse of the other, it's not a good habit to get into—in my opinion, hammers have no place around bearings. Once the bearings are out, test them by spinning them with your hand. If the grease is dry, the bearing will spin and even coast for a while; if it's really bad, you'll feel flat spots in the bearing.

Replacement bearings are easy to obtain. Each bearing will have a shield number on one or both sides, which should be all the information a bearing supplier will need to get you a replacement. For instance, a 2802Z would be a double-row bearing that presses into a $1\frac{3}{8}$-in. bearing seat and accepts a $\frac{5}{8}$-in. shaft. Bearing suppliers are listed

1. Fit the tenon on the pusher block inside the hollow shaft (below left).
2. Insert the spindle and bearing into the support block and align the bench dog on the pusher block. Use the shoulder vise to push the spindle out of the bearing (top right, bottom left).
3. The bearing removed from the spindle.
4. To replace the bearing on the spindle, use the shoulder vise to force the spindle into the bearing (bottom left).

If you have a European-style workbench, it's not difficult to improvise an arbor press. Using the bench dogs in combination with two turned pieces of wood will provide the necessary force you need to remove the bearings from the spindle.

To make the support block for the spindle, mount a square block in a four-jaw chuck and drill a hole through it to a diameter slightly larger than the spindle (1⅛ in. for the spindle assembly in the photos). Then scrape a pocket in the support block to accept the bearing.

To make the pusher block, turn a hickory block to a tenon with a shoulder. The tenon diameter should be equal to the inside diameter of the shaft. Clamp the support block to the workbench, insert the tenon into the spindle, then use the shoulder vise to force the spindle out of the bearing, as shown in the photos above.

in the Yellow Pages (Bearing Distributors and Bearings, Inc., are two of the better-known companies). It never hurts to take the bearing along with you to the bearing store, so you can check the replacement directly against the original. You'll be amazed at just how inexpensive a new set of bearings is—typically no more than $15.

Once you have the new bearings for your lathe, reassemble the spindle assembly and headstock in the reverse order that you took it apart. The correct sequence for reinstalling the bearings on the Delta 46-700 is shown in the photo essay on p. 148.

In the rare event that you have a very old set of bearings for which replacements are no longer available, you may still be able to salvage the bearings. Such bearings are typically shielded with a metal disc on one side but not sealed. Once you have the bearings out of the headstock, soak them in kerosene or a similar solvent (in a well-ventilated area) to remove the old, dried grease and dirt. Never use compressed air on bearings since it usually ruins them. A soft brush and some elbow grease will remove the dirt just fine.

Next, heat up some grease in a metal can. Use an electric hot plate, and be most careful of fire—I prefer to do this kind of work outside. Almost any good-quality automotive grease will work, but if you're a stickler for doing it right, you can get tubes of grease specially formulated for bearings at any bearing store. Drop the bearings in the liquid grease and let them soak for a while. Once the grease cools, pull the bearings out, remove the excess, and you're back in business.

Although it's not a difficult job to replace bearings, not everyone has the proper tools for it. The best alternative to doing it yourself is to take the entire headstock to an automotive machine shop and have the work done for you. Automotive machine shops abound, and they're well equipped for any work involving bearing removal and replacement. On most lathes, the headstock is a separate piece and can be removed. If the headstock and bed are a one-piece casting, you'll have to take the entire machine to the shop.

Installing new bearings

1. Put the new bearings and spindle back in the headstock casting, then replace the snap ring that retains the rear bearing.

2. Replace the front bearing, which is a slide fit with the spindle. Note the wavy washer that goes between the snap ring and the bearing to take up play.

3. Replace the snap ring after the wavy washer.

4. Thread the nut onto the spindle nose and up against the inner bearing race. The outside face of this nut creates a shoulder for the faceplate.

Drive pulleys, belts and motors

Drive pulleys and belts can give a good deal of trouble, even in new lathes. If a lathe has "as cast" die-cast pulleys (which are common on economy lathes), chances are that they are neither perfectly concentric nor round. Since V-belts grip on the flanks of the pulley groove, a dial indicator is of little or no use in checking accuracy. The best method is to turn the pulleys over by hand with a pointer held stationary in the groove. A pointed object such as a scriber can be clamped in a suitable place near the pulley. Any radial or side-to-side runout will be apparent through careful observation. Concentricity tolerances for pulleys are quite loose—usually 0.005-in. to 0.006-in. minimum runout. If the runout is excessive (over 0.010 in.) and your lathe is having vibration problems, the pulley is the likely culprit.

What you should do about pulleys that are out of true will depend largely on how much money you want to spend and how much trouble you're willing to go to. The best solution is to replace the defective pulleys with machined cast-iron models, which should last as long as your lathe. High-quality pulleys to fit most spindles are available at most bearing stores, but they'll be expensive ($30 to $60 each) and have to be special-ordered. If your headstock spindle is an odd size, you may still have to have the arbor hole bored out and the keyway broached.

Isolating vibration

Vibration is a problem that can cause great consternation, since turning is difficult if the machine and work are moving around. Vibration tends to be speed related—most lathes have a bit of vibration, usually at one or two specific speeds. This is one of the reasons I like variable speed. If the work itself is causing the vibration, tweaking the speed up or down a bit is an instant cure.

Pulleys and belts are the most common sources of vibration, and these are the first things to inspect. Check for worn belts and out-of-true pulleys. If these are in good shape, next check the dynamic balance of the rotating parts. The motor may even be out of balance; although this isn't a common problem, it does happen.

Vibration is often a problem on lathes that have sheet-metal stands. Pouring sand into the stand can work wonders, but you have to make sure that the sand doesn't get into the motor, pulleys or other moving parts. (If you're pouring sand into the stand, make sure you leave some air space below the motor for cooling purposes.) Placing sand bags in the base of the machine will often do the trick. Stamped-metal legs can be reinforced by adding wood cross braces, and vibration can be dampened by draping sand bags over the cross members. Another alternative is to build a replacement plywood box stand for your lathe and fill the legs with sand (see the photo on p. 22).

Another remedy is to have the die-cast pulleys machined by a local machine shop. I've also mounted die-cast pulleys in a wood lathe and machined the sides of the grooves with a scraper. This is the same kind of work as modifying a faceplate (see pp. 40-41). I mount a suitable square of wood in a four-jaw scroll chuck such as the Nova or the Oneway (see p. 43). I then turn the end to a short stub arbor that's a press fit with the pulley. I push the pulley on the arbor and lock it there with the setscrew in the pulley, as shown in the photo essay on the facing page. I now start the lathe and scrape the offending groove flanks true. It's really quite simple; however, since your lathe is apart there are some technical problems to overcome—you'll either have to do the work on a second lathe, or temporarily substitute a simple one-groove pulley for the one you're scraping.

Sometimes dirt and rubber from the belt will build up in the pulley grooves and cause the belt to make a "klunking" sound as it runs. This buildup can usually be removed with solvent, but sometimes it will require sanding or filing. Again, mounting the pulley on a stub arbor can help in this task. Finally, a pulley greatly out of balance can cause excessive vibration. Many automotive machine shops have dynamic balancing machines and can remedy the problem for you. For the headstock pulley, have both the spindle and the pulley balanced as a unit.

Belts are much like tires, ranging greatly in price and quality. The difference between discount-store belts and good belts is like the difference between bias-ply tires and radial tires. A cheap belt will be stiff and uneven in cross-section and will often cause noise and vibration. You can obtain a high-quality replacement belt from a bearing store for less than $10; Gates Green Belts are a reliable brand. It's good shop practice to replace the belt whenever you replace the bearings and vice versa. You can usually expect to get two to five years of use out of a good belt (less if your lathe has a variable-speed drive).

The motor that powers your lathe can sometimes require attention. When faced with a motor that won't run, you have two options: repair it or replace it. Your nose will usually tell you if the motor is burned out—it will have a distinct electrical-fire smell. Unless the motor is underpowered to begin with, rewinding is usually a good option. A motor rewinder (look in the Yellow Pages) can rebuild the motor for between $100 and $150. A rewinder can also help with other motor ills. Common problems with single-phase induction motors are burned-out starting winding, problems with the centrifugal starting switch or a bad capacitor.

Truing a die-cast pulley

1. Mount the pulley on a stub arbor that has been turned from a square of hickory in a four-jaw scroll chuck.

2. Secure the pulley on the stub arbor by locking the setscrew.

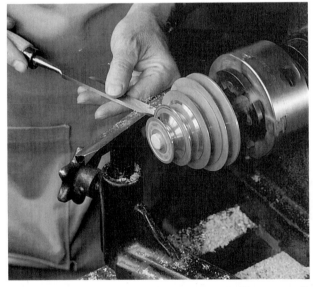

3. Use a woodturning scraper ground to the correct shape to true the pulley grooves.

Removing seized Morse tapers and faceplates

It's not uncommon for a Morse-taper accessory to become stuck in the headstock or tailstock spindle. This typically occurs when you slam a Morse taper hard into the socket when the spindle is hot after a bout of high-speed turning. The hot socket shrinks around the cold Morse-taper center. Running the lathe until it heats up again usually cures the problem, but if this doesn't work, more drastic measures are necessary.

The correct way to remove a Morse taper is to insert a knockout bar through the back of the spindle and drive it out with a snap of the wrist. If the Morse taper is stuck, however, repeated blows with a knockout bar will do no more than put flat spots in the bearings. The problem here is overcoming starting friction, and the best course of action is to get a heavy hammer and give the knockout bar one firm blow (which does less damage to the bearings than a series of light raps). Once you have overcome starting friction, the rest of the force from your hammer blow goes into propelling the taper out of the spindle at high velocity. Have your other hand ready to catch the taper, or, if you're unsure of your catching abilities, hold a scrap board against it. For tapers seized in self-ejecting tailstocks, the spindle has to be removed so that a knockout bar can be placed against the taper.

A faceplate can also become frozen on the spindle thread. A common cause is not threading a heavily loaded plate all the way home when initially mounting it on the lathe. When the lathe is started the faceplate is screwed home with tremendous force. There are a number of remedies for this problem, the first being simply to get a bigger wrench. More leverage can be obtained by using a "cheater," which is a short length of pipe that is slipped over the handle of the wrench. Where possible, rest the wrench for the spindle against the lathe bed or headstock casting to provide a rock-solid stop. If the cheater doesn't work, try hitting the wrench directly with a couple of blows from a lead or brass hammer.

If the above methods fail, you'll have to resort to harsher remedies. Place a heavy brass bar against one flat of the faceplate nut and give it a sharp rap with a hammer. The idea is to give the threaded portion of the faceplate a shocking blow at right angles to the axis of the thread, which will break up the molecular interaction between the two threads. Go back to the wrenches and the faceplate will usually come right off.

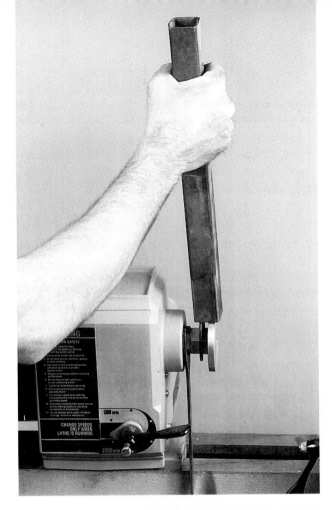

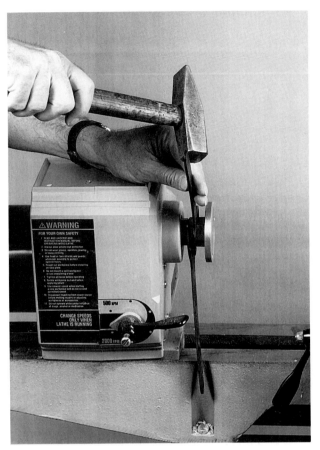

If a faceplate gets stuck, remove it by using a 'cheater' bar over the spindle wrench (above left). If this doesn't work, hitting the wrench lightly with a hammer usually cures the problem (above). Finally, hammering a brass drift against one flat of the faceplate nut (left) will usually undo the most tenacious of faceplates.

In the unlikely event that no mechanical means will remove the seized faceplate, one final remedy is to use a propane torch to heat one flat of the threaded area (wear heavy leather gloves for this operation). It's important to heat only one small area of the plate, which will cause the circumference to expand much as if you form a circle with your thumb and index finger then push the two slightly apart at the tips. Avoid heating the spindle and bearings as much as possible. When the plate is hot, use a wrench to remove it.

Tool rests

Tool rests are subject to heavy wear during everyday turning and will benefit from occasional re-dressing. It's surprising to realize one day that there is a definite low spot in the center of your metal rest, to say nothing of a multitude of nicks and dents. The best tool for removing these imperfections is a large single-cut mill file in either bastard or first cut (a double-cut file will not work for this process). Draw-file the rest by turning the file sideways and alternately pulling and pushing it over the rest, much as if it were a spokeshave. You'll be rewarded with long ribbons of steel or iron.

Draw filing also allows you to reshape a rest to your own needs. No two manufacturers make their rest quite the same, and the best edge shape is a matter of considerable debate. The drawing on the facing page shows my personal preference for a tool-rest shape. This design places the fulcrum point close to the work for good leverage and offers good support of the tool in all types of turning (unlike rests of flatter design).

Although the standard tool rest that comes with your lathe is adequate for most turning operations, it's worth making special tool rests to speed up production work. Tool rests are quite easy to fabricate from structural steel. Use a short length of cold rolled steel of the appropriate diameter for the neck and braze or weld a piece of flat stock to it at the proper angle. Once the rest is welded, draw-file the top to the desired shape. If you don't have welding equipment, any welder can do the job for you at a nominal price. I've made 18-in. long rests in this way, as well as odd-shaped rests for special situations. A handy shape is an S-curve: it allows you to turn the inside of a bowl from one end of the rest and the outside from the opposite end.

You can also make an excellent tool rest of considerable length out of wood. Extended wooden rests were a favorite among High Wycombe turners. To make the rest, mount a stepped pin in the tool base and a

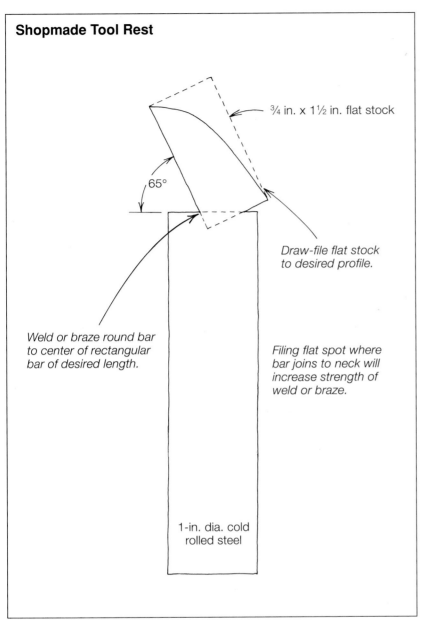

Shopmade Tool Rest

¾ in. x 1½ in. flat stock

65°

Draw-file flat stock to desired profile.

Weld or braze round bar to center of rectangular bar of desired length.

Filing flat spot where bar joins to neck will increase strength of weld or braze.

1-in. dia. cold rolled steel

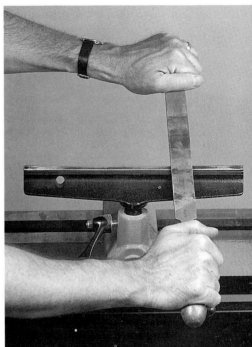

Use a single-cut mill file to true the edge of a tool rest.

right-angle support bracket on the tailstock (see the photos on p. 156). You should be able to find a good solid spot to drill and tap a ⅜-in. x 16 threads per inch (TPI) hole on most tailstocks. I cut the head off a standard ⅜-in. x 16 TPI carriage bolt and bend it at right angles to make the bracket. If possible, heat the bolt to cherry red at the point you want to bend it (you can bend the bolt cold, but it may break). Use a solid hardwood such as oak or maple for the rest itself, and drill holes on the underside to mount on the pin and bracket. Shape the desired edge profile with a spokeshave.

Building an extended wooden tool rest makes it possible to work along the entire length of a turning without having to reposition the rest. This tool rest mounts on a pin in the tool base and a right-angle bracket in the tailstock.

A full-length rest is great for turning table legs and other spindles, because the entire piece can be turned without having to move the rest. Wood rests do wear fairly quickly, but a couple of passes with a spokeshave will restore the profile. If you're using a wood rest for repetitive production work, the indented spots at the very edge formed where you roll coves and beads can be an aid to duplication. The dents don't inhibit the use of the roughing-out gouge and the skew, because these tools will ride at a point just behind the edge (and the dents), at least if you form the top of the rest to my suggested design.

Modifying a lathe

Now and again a job will come along that's just a bit beyond the capacity of your lathe. For want of a couple inches of swing, you end up modifying the entire project to make the one turning slightly smaller. One way to get around this problem is to increase the swing of your lathe. As long as the headstock is a separate piece (not cast as part of the bed) you can unbolt it and interpose a couple of wood blocks to raise it up. You'll have to find a longer bolt or bolts to hold it down, and there is a definite limit to how much you can raise things up—usually about 1 in. on smaller lathes and up to 2 in. on larger machines.

Swing is increased by double these amounts. If you need to use the tailstock, block it up in the same way. (A word of caution: Make sure you run your new blocked-up lathe at low speed.)

It's also possible to stretch a lathe so you can turn long work such as porch columns and canopy-bed posts. Bench lathes are quite easy to stretch. Simply bolt the bed to a plank of suitable length, then bolt the tailstock to a block at the end of the plank that raises it to the proper height. For floor-model lathes, bolt a suitable wood extension to the bed, or the tailstock to a bench or table nearby. Remember that exact center alignment is of no great importance in spindle turning. With either setup, stretch a wooden tool rest (see above) from the tool base to the tailstock.

Restoring a used lathe

Corrosion can be a chronic problem with lathes, and chances are that if you buy an old lathe it will have some rust. To restore the machine to its former glory, you can use the buffers described on pp. 75-78. A spiral-sewn wheel with emery compound will make quick work of light rust on the exterior surfaces. Small parts can be removed and taken to the buffer. For larger areas such as the bed ways, mount the 4-in. arbor buff in an electric drill and bring it to the lathe.

Emery paper and steel wool are also good weapons in the war on rust. For extremely heavy rusting with pitting, various proprietary preparations, often referred to as "naval jelly," work well. They loosen the surface rust and change the chemical nature of the rust in the pits, thereby preventing further rusting.

For the best finish for your used lathe, brush on one or more coats of machinery enamel (available from any hardware or paint store). It's best to remove any bolts and screws possible and to mask areas such as name plates and bed ways with masking tape. Once the paint dries, remove the masking tape, replace the bolts and screws, and you have a classic restoration. To maintain your newly restored lathe (or any lathe) and prevent future rusting, get into the habit of wiping down the exterior surfaces with a rag on a regular basis, and always apply a thin film of paste wax to the bed after a turning session with green wood.

Finding missing parts for classic lathes

Finding a missing part for an otherwise great classic lathe can present a problem, since the manufacturer may have gone out of business long ago. Although want-ads in woodworking magazines can yield results, you'll often have to buy an entire lathe to get the part you need. Having the part made at a machine shop is usually the best alternative, and prices can be quite reasonable—$50 to $100 for a part such as a spindle, pulley or tailstock wheel. If you're considering buying a lathe that's missing major parts, such as a tailstock, check around before buying. Such a lathe is not worth much unless the manufacturer is still in business and parts are available.

CHAPTER 6
Projects

As a conclusion to this book, I've come up with three turning projects that will serve as a review of the information on tools and techniques outlined in earlier chapters. The first project, a Queen Anne finial, is a simple spindle turning. The second, a drawer pull, is a simple faceplate exercise. The third, a Windsor stool, entails both faceplate and spindle work.

I've included a drawing for each project and a series of photos that illustrate the tools and techniques you should use, and in what order. Even if you decide not to make the projects, the illustrations will help you understand how to apply the information that has come before. However, I do strongly encourage you to complete the projects, since it's only through practice that turning proficiency can be gained.

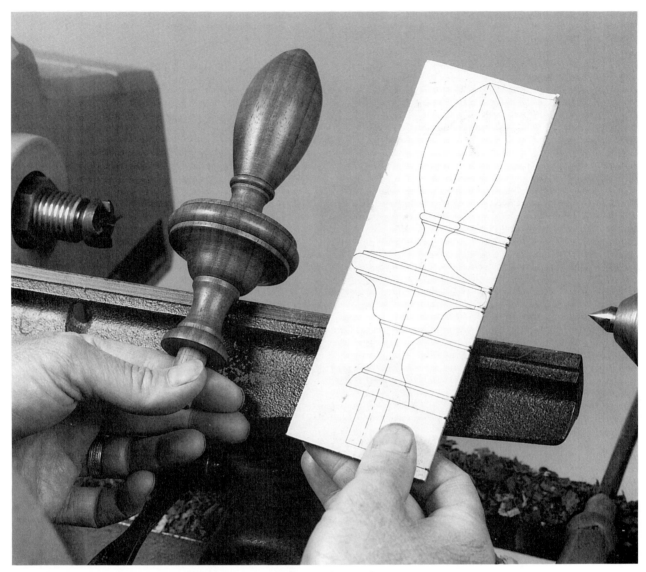

This Queen Anne finial is a straightforward spindle-turning project, turned with coves and beads and requiring the use of a pattern stick.

Project 1: A Queen Anne finial

The first project is a finial for a Queen Anne bonnet-top highboy. I got the idea from Norman Vandal's book *Queen Anne Furniture* (The Taunton Press, 1990), where you can find detailed instructions for making the entire chest of drawers. The finial is a straightforward between-centers spindle-turning project, turned with coves and beads and requiring the use of a pattern stick, as described in Chapter 4.

1. Begin by drawing the finial at full scale on the face of the pattern stick. Then mount the starting billet between centers in the lathe (the photo shows a piece of walnut 2^{11}/$_{16}$ in. square and 8^1/$_2$ in. long).

2. Use a 1^1/$_2$-in. roughing-out gouge to bring the billet round.

Project 1: Queen Anne Finial

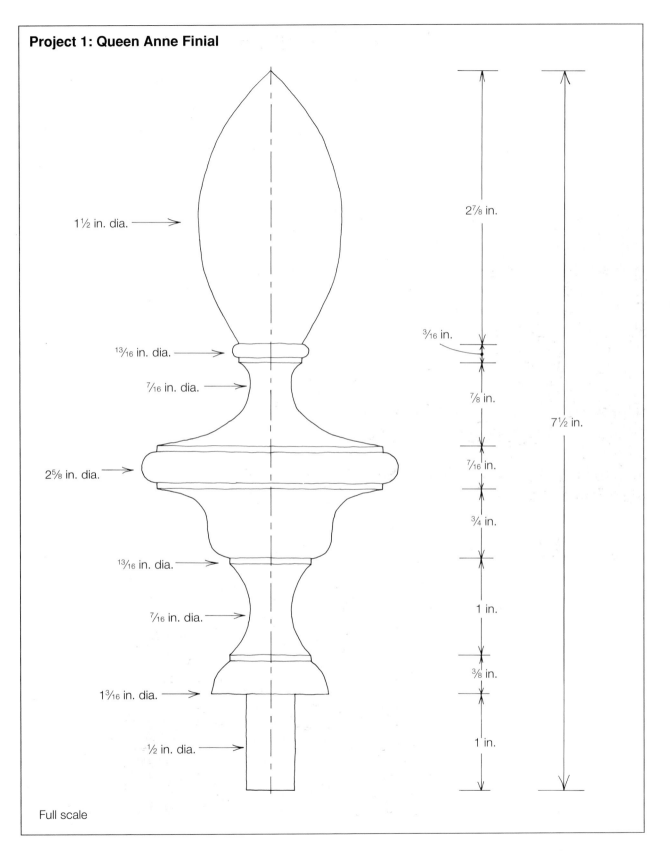

1½ in. dia.

¹³⁄₁₆ in. dia.

⁷⁄₁₆ in. dia.

2⅝ in. dia.

¹³⁄₁₆ in. dia.

⁷⁄₁₆ in. dia.

1³⁄₁₆ in. dia.

½ in. dia.

2⅞ in.

³⁄₁₆ in.

⅞ in.

⁷⁄₁₆ in.

¾ in.

1 in.

⅜ in.

1 in.

7½ in.

Full scale

3. Touch your fingers against the back of the work to feel when it just comes round.

4. Once the work is round, use a 1-in. skew chisel to produce a perfect cylinder.

5. Square the ends of the cylinder with a ½-in. spindle gouge. Use it on its side (flute pointing toward the tailstock) with the bevel rubbing. Avoid touching the spinning center, for this will dull the tool.

6. Balance the pattern on the tool rest and transfer the critical points to the spinning work. Holding a pencil in notches cut in the edge of the pattern stick allows precise spacing of the elements.

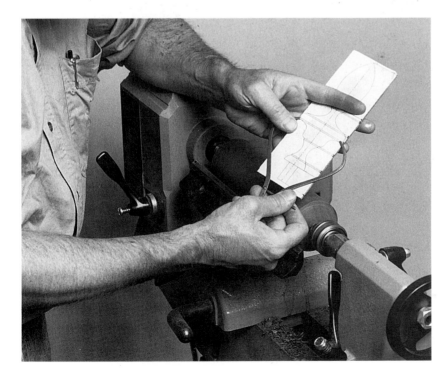

7. Set a pair of calipers to size the shoulders of the first bead, the top of which is the major diameter on the finial. (Remember that to minimize harmonic chatter, you should always turn the thickest part of the spindle first and the thinnest part last.) All the secondary diameters are sized in the same way.

8. Use an ⅛-in. diamond-section parting tool to turn the shoulder of the first bead. When the calipers just drop over the work, you know you're at the correct diameter.

9. Turn the other shoulder of the bead in the same way to create a rondel from which the bead will be turned.

10. Use a ½-in. spindle gouge to complete the first bead.

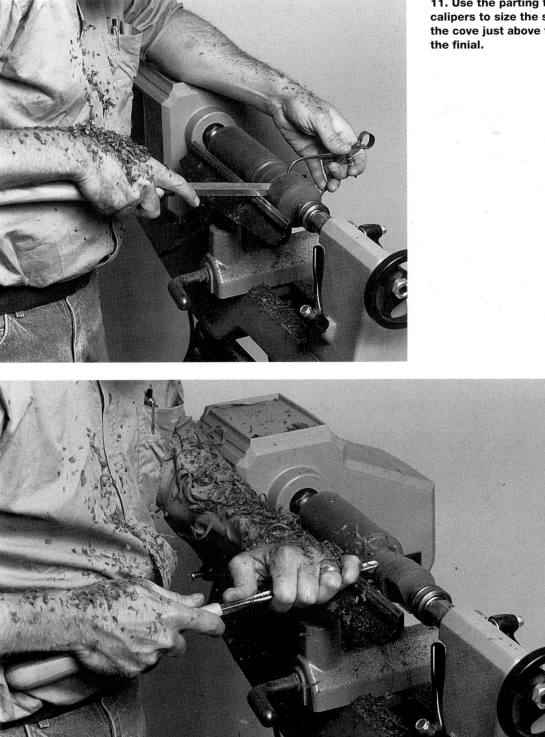

11. Use the parting tool and calipers to size the shoulders of the cove just above the base of the finial.

12. Turn the S-curve between the major bead and the shoulder of the cove with the ½-in. spindle gouge.

13. Cut the cove just above the base of the finial.

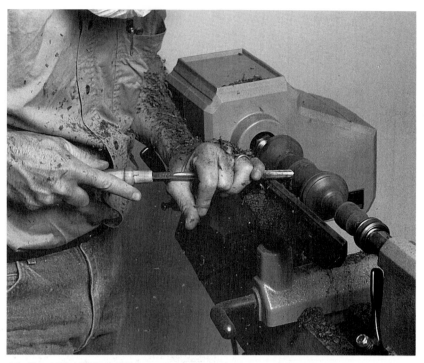

14. Turn the flame to a gentle curve up to the small bead at its base.

15. Clean up the shoulder of the major bead.

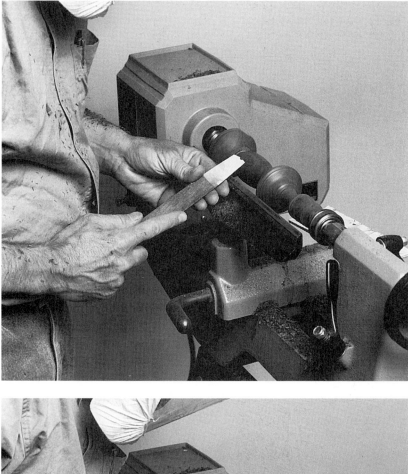

16. The bead at the base of the finial is too small to cut consistently with a gouge by eye, and a tool rest cannot be brought close to it. To get around these problems, grind the edge of an old file to the profile of the small bead and use this 'form tool' (see pp. 120-121) to scrape the slope on the flame adjacent to the bead, the bead itself and the shoulder below it.

17. Scrape the small bead, holding the form tool downhill.

18. Turn the lower profile of the flame to meet up with and match the cut made by the form tool.

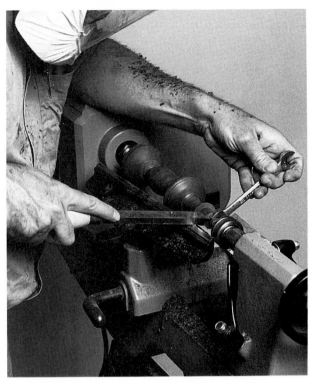

19. Use a ½-in. open-end wrench to size the tenon that will secure the finial to the top of the highboy.

20. Holding the open-end wrench in your left hand, use the parting tool to turn the tenon to the correct diameter.

21. Remove the tool rest and, with the lathe running, hold a small piece of sandpaper against the back of the work. Begin with 180 grit and work up through 220 grit for a smooth finish.

22. For a fine French polish finish, pad shellac onto the work...

23. ...and burnish with shavings. French polish brings out the natural beauty of the wood and is both transparent and durable. It's also a good sanding sealer for most other finishes.

24. Part off by turning the flame away to nothing with a ½-in. spindle gouge.

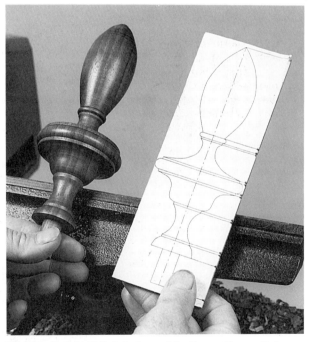

25. The finished finial alongside the pattern stick.

Project 2: A drawer pull

This drawer pull is a whimsical knob of my own design. The design is such that it can be faceplate turned or spindle turned, though most knobs are face work to provide the strongest grain direction. The dot of contrasting wood is a personal signature that I like to put on my best furniture.

I save pieces of highly figured wood for knobs. There are always cutoffs, often from the actual project I'm making the knob for. For this project, I chose a piece of soft maple burl I had lying about. Bandsaw cubes of the appropriate size for the knobs you plan to make. For this knob, I used a starting cube just a tad over 1⅜ in. square by 2 in. long. The cube is mounted on the shopmade screw chuck described on pp. 47-48. The advantages of using this chuck are that the screw matches the one that will be used to install the knob and the chuck can be turned to the diameter of the base of the knob. The latter makes duplication of the base diameter simple because it has only to match the chuck. If the tool touches the chuck, there is no harm done.

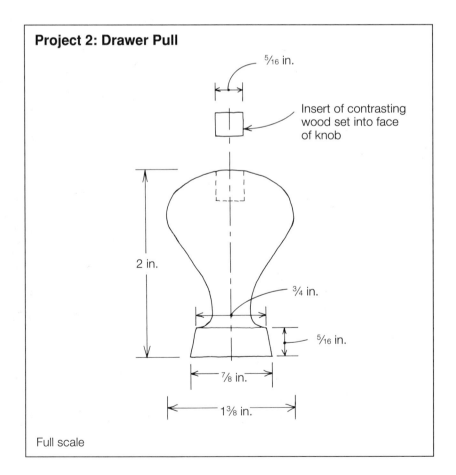

Project 2: Drawer Pull

⁵⁄₁₆ in.

Insert of contrasting wood set into face of knob

2 in.

¾ in.

⁵⁄₁₆ in.

⅞ in.

1⅜ in.

Full scale

1. Mount the starting billet on a shopmade screw chuck.

2. Use a ¼-in. bowl gouge to turn the work to 1⅜ in. diameter along its whole length.

3. Turn the base of the knob to the diameter of the chuck.

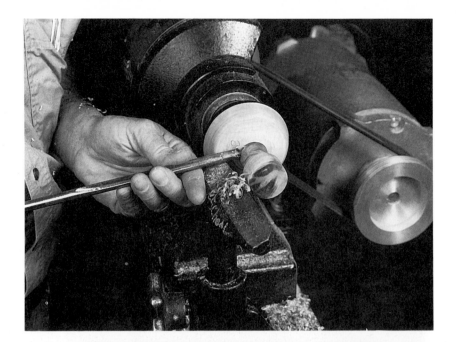

4. Turn the cove between the base of the knob and the major diameter.

5. Reposition the tool rest and turn the face of the knob.

6. With the tool rest removed, sand the knob, working from 80 grit through 220 grit.

7. French polish is a good, durable finish for knobs. Use a small rag to apply the shellac, then burnish with shavings and crayon on some carnauba wax.

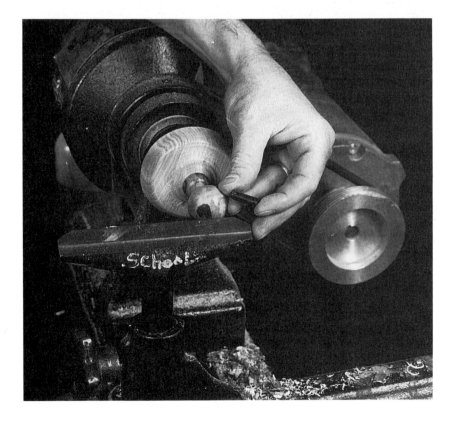

8. At this stage you have a fine knob in its own right, but I like to add a dot of contrasting wood for extra pizzazz. For the insert in this knob, I spindle-turned a piece of ebony between centers to a diameter of ⁵⁄₁₆ in. (using an open-end wrench to check the diameter).

9. Use a ¼-in. spindle gouge to drill a small starting hole at the center of the knob. The trick is to turn the gouge 90° counterclockwise from horizontal and present it straight into the center of the work. Alternatively, you can use a drill in the tailstock for this task.

10. An inexpensive screwdriver makes a good scraper for scraping out the starting hole to a press fit with the ⁵⁄₁₆-in. insert.

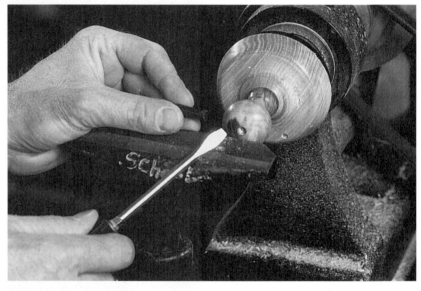

11. Gently tap the ebony inlay into place with a hammer.

12. After backsawing the excess away, use a ¼-in. spindle gouge to turn the insert flush.

13. The finished knob (with the shopmade screw chuck in the background).

Project 3: A Windsor stool

The final project is a four-legged Windsor stool designed by my good friend Michael Dunbar. (If you want to know more about Windsor chairs, I recommend you read his book *Make a Windsor Chair with Michael Dunbar,* The Taunton Press, 1984.) It's a most pleasant (and handy) stool, with a deeply dished and commodious 14-in. diameter seat that's very comfortable. The seat is about 20 in. high and can be lowered by changing the splay of the legs. This height is a little higher than normal seating, but it's very convenient for some tasks—such as typing at a table. I prefer a little less splay than was common in an 18th-century Windsor chair, and my design reflects that preference. The legs and stretchers are simple double and single bobbins that are easy to duplicate.

Windsor stools were common in 18th- and 19th-century America. The seat would have been made from pine or tulip poplar and the legs from riven green maple or birch. If you make the stool from these woods, dry the tenons out in a household oven set at 100° to 150° or in hot sand before final turning (you can heat a pan of sand on the stove and push the tenon area into the sand for an hour or so). The completed stool would have been finished with milk paint. You can also turn the stool from kiln-dried maple and give it a modern finish, which was my original plan. When I arrived at my lumber dealer, he didn't have a single board of 8/4 maple. I had to settle for curly maple, which he sold me at soft-maple price, and that made my heart jump.

1. Hand-plane a suitable piece of 8/4 stock for the seat of the stool.

Project 3: Windsor Stool

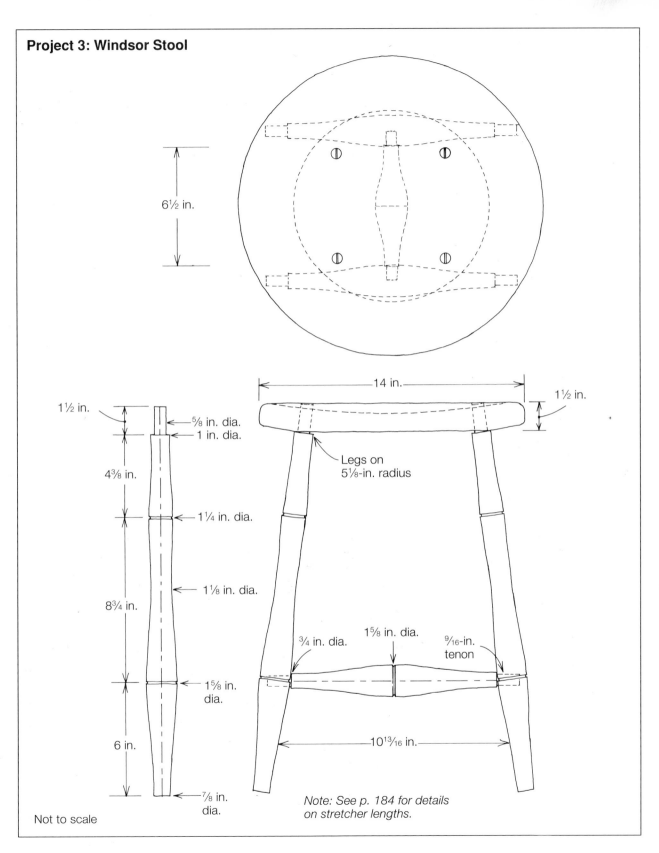

6½ in.

14 in.

1½ in.

1½ in.

⁵⁄₈ in. dia.
1 in. dia.

4³⁄₈ in.

1¼ in. dia.

1⅛ in. dia.

8¾ in.

Legs on
5⅛-in. radius

¾ in. dia.

1⅝ in. dia.

⁹⁄₁₆-in.
tenon

1⅝ in.
dia.

6 in.

10¹³⁄₁₆ in.

⁷⁄₈ in.
dia.

Not to scale

*Note: See p. 184 for details
on stretcher lengths.*

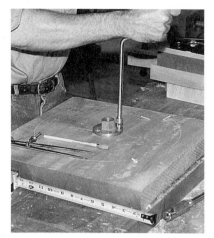

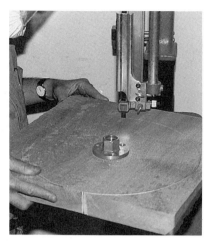

2. Use a pair of dividers to lay out the 14-in. çircle for the seat.

3. Attach a faceplate to the blank with hex-head sheet-metal screws. The center point left by the dividers will aid in centering the faceplate.

4. Bandsaw the seat round.

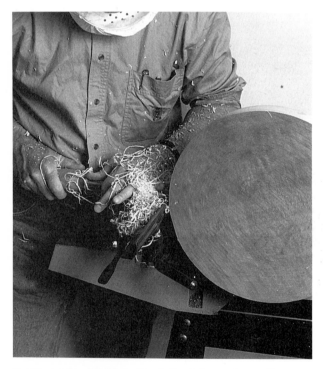

5. Mount the blank in the lathe (shown here, the Delta 46-700), with the headstock swung out for outboard turning. Use a ½-in. bowl gouge to true up the outside diameter.

6. Cutting a taper on the underside of the seat thins the edge and makes it more visually appealing. The taper should start just outside the circle the leg holes are laid out on and extend to the edge (see the drawing of the stool on p. 177).

7. Turn the seat from its original 2-in. thickness to a final thickness of 1½ in., then use the same bowl gouge to dish the seat. Work from the perimeter in. If tool marks are a problem, use a large dome scraper to smooth the final contour to the seat.

8. Use a straightedge to check the dish of the seat.

9. Use a disc sander with a contour pad to sand the seat.

10. Mount the billet (1¹¹⁄₁₆ in. square by 20⅝ in. long) for the first leg between centers.

11. Using a roughing-out gouge, turn the center area round so that a steady rest can be brought into play. (Steady rests help overcome harmonic chatter when turning long spindles.)

12. The steady rest (made of Baltic-birch plywood) in position. Note the rubber bands used to keep pressure on the wedge.

13. Use a roughing-out gouge to rough-shape the leg and cut the gentle curve and taper.

14. Establish the center of each bobbin from pencil marks on the full-length wood tool rest. These marks will help you duplicate the other three legs for the stool.

15. Use a ¼-in. spindle gouge to turn the small cove at the center of the lower bobbin. (The bobbin diameter is established by just bringing the 1¹¹⁄₁₆-in. square billet round.)

16. Use a parting tool and calipers to size the upper bobbin, which is 1¼ in. in diameter.

17. Use a roughing-out gouge to finish the tapers adjacent to the bobbins.

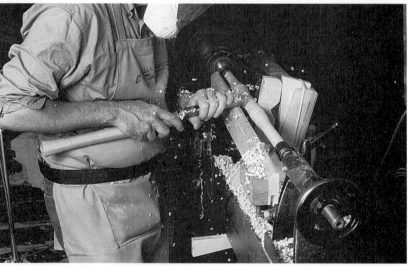

18. Size the ⅝-in. diameter tenon with an open-end wrench. If turning green wood, turn the tenon ⅛ in. to ¼ in. oversize, then turn to final size after drying in hot sand or a household oven.

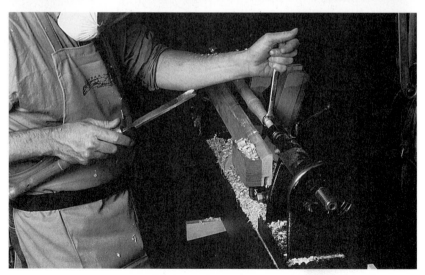

19. Lightly sand and French-polish the leg before removing it from the lathe.

20. The first leg finished.

21. Once you have turned the first leg, the others will be easy to duplicate. Use the marks on the tool rest as a layout guide and the first leg itself as a visual reference.

22. Use a bevel as a sight-line gauge to angle the hole for the leg. The amount of splay is a matter of taste. If possible, have a helper hold the legs at various angles while you look at the stool from a distance. Drill with a ⅝-in. brad-point bit until the point just breaks out.

23. To ensure that the hole will emerge from the top of the seat with no chipping, turn the seat over and drill from the breakout hole.

24. Dry-assemble the legs, then measure the distance between the lower bobbins for the two side stretchers. Add ¼ in. to this measurement and 1 in. extra at each end for the tenons. Cut two 1¹¹⁄₁₆-in. square billets to exact length and turn the side stretchers with single bobbins.

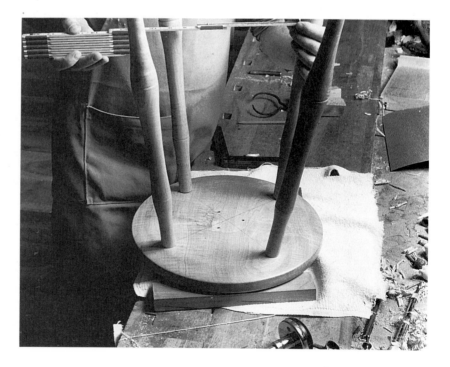

25. Measure the distance for the middle stretcher, again adding 2¼ in.

26. Assemble the stool with glue on all tenons. Because the stretchers were all cut ¼ in. long, the stool assembles under compression. For additional stability, fox-wedge the seat tenons for a never-fail fit. Be sure to wedge across the seat grain so that the seat fibers are stretched—wedging with the grain can split the seat. Cut the tenons flush with the seat using a fishtail gouge.

27. Apply some French polish to the seat...

28. ...and your Windsor stool is complete.

GLOSSARY

Bead
A raised, convex ridge on the surface of a turning.

Beading-and-parting tool
A very small double-bevel chisel that can be used for turning beads. It's also useful for sizing tenons and, in combination with calipers, for sizing work. The inclusive grind angle between the two bevels is usually about 42°.

Bed
The rail-like platform on which the headstock, tailstock and tool base mount. The two strips that form the rails are called ways and are made of wood, cast iron or structural steel. The tailstock and tool base are easily slid back and forth on the ways but can be locked fast as necessary.

Bedan
A single-bevel chisel that is used much the same as the beading-and-parting tool. The bevel is ground to about 30°.

Bevel
The ground face of a turning tool that forms the cutting edge.

Bowl gouge
A gouge for faceplate work. It has an asymmetrical flute, and the bevel is ground to a variety of forms depending on the turning situation.

Bowl lathe
A very short bed lathe, often without a tailstock, that is used exclusively for faceplate work. Its name derives from its popularity with bowl turners.

Catch
The nick that occurs when the tool edge digs into the work after control is lost.

Centerline
A line along the edge of the work at the same height as the centers (not to be confused with the true centerline, which lies along the longitudinal axis of the workpiece). This would be at 9 o'clock when viewing the work from the tailstock end.

Chatter work
Decorative patterns created in the end grain by a small scraping tool of thin section, presented in such a way that it vibrates at a given frequency to create the pattern. *See also* Harmonic chatter.

Clearance angle
The angle between the bevel of a tool and the surface of the work.

Collet chuck
A metal chuck with a slotted cylinder that can be tightened around the work or expanded inside the work.

Cove
A U-shaped depression cut into the surface of a workpiece. It is the opposite shape to the bead.

Cup center
A device with a center point on a Morse-taper shank of the appropriate size with a raised ridge around it (also called a "ring center"). It allows the tailstock to hold the work, both radially and axially.

Cup chuck
See Jam chuck.

Cutoff tool.
See Parting tool.

Dead center
A cup or 60° center that mounts in the tailstock spindle to hold work. It does not spin with the work, hence its name. It both holds the work radially and acts as the bearing on which the work rotates.

Dressing
The act of refacing a grinding wheel to make it round and bring fresh, sharp grinding particles to the surface. This is done with a diamond or star-wheel dresser.

Drill chuck
See Jacobs chuck.

Drive/spur center
A center on a Morse-taper shank of the appropriate size with a central point surrounded by two or four sharp tines that engage the work.

Duplicator
A mechanical device that mounts on a lathe and allows you to copy any turned workpiece.

Faceplate
A cast-iron, steel or aluminum-alloy disc that can be threaded onto the headstock spindle. There are one or more circles of holes around the periphery for screws to hold work to the surface of the plate.

Faceplate turning
Any turning situation in which the grain of the work is at right angles to the axis of the lathe bed.

Flute
A cove that runs the length of a spindle turning rather than around it. Also the concave groove along the shaft of a turning tool.

Form tool
A scraper ground to a specific form. It allows convenient duplication of the shape, and in some instances will make cuts that are not possible with any other tool.

Gap
A dip in the bed just in front of the headstock on some lathes. It allows faceplate work of greater swing to be mounted in this area.

Ghost
The hard-to-distinguish pattern created by the corners of the work spinning in the lathe before it is round. Seeing the ghost is an important part of turning from square to round.

Glue block
A disc of wood slightly larger than the faceplate that is glued to the work for chucking.

Grind angle
The inclusive angle from the back of a tool to the bevel.

Harmonic chatter
A spiral pattern in spindle work caused when the work becomes thin enough to vibrate.

Headstock
The heart of the lathe. It contains the spindle and assorted bearings. Pulleys on the spindle are belted to the motor. The spindle nose is threaded for faceplates and usually has a Morse-taper socket.

High Wycombe lathe
A wood-bed lathe peculiar to the High Wycombe area of England. It was popular with the bodgers who turned furniture parts in the forests in that area. Today, any wood-bed lathe is referred to as a High Wycombe lathe.

Hollow grind
The hollowing of a tool bevel produced by the convex surface of the grinding wheel.

Index head
A mechanism that locks the headstock spindle at regularly spaced intervals so that layout or auxiliary operations with a router can be performed.

Interrupted cut
A cut made on work that is not perfectly round. The tool is cutting the work some of the time and cutting air the rest. Needless to say, the tool is much more difficult to control in an interrupted cut.

Jacobs chuck
A key-type three-jaw chuck for holding drills in the headstock or tailstock.

Jam chuck
A wooden chuck, made on a faceplate, that resembles a cup. The work is held in a tapered pocket scraped into the interior of the cup.

Laying grain down
Cutting downhill on the grain.

Live center
A tailstock center, either cup or 60°, that has bearings so that it can turn with the work.

Morse taper
A system of tapers (about 3° inclusive) that allow accessories to be mounted in the headstock or tailstock spindle.

Offset turning
A turning situation where the workpiece is offset from the original starting center at one or both ends. (The crankshaft of a car is turned in this way.)

Outboard turning
A situation where faceplate work is not turned over the bed of the lathe. On some lathes, the headstock swivels so that the work spins in front of the bed. On others, the back end of the headstock spindle is left-hand threaded to receive a special faceplate.

Paper joint
A glue joint in which kraft paper is interposed in the glue line. This allows a spindle turning to be divided lengthwise into two, four or more pieces. It also can be used for faceplate turnings and as a chucking method to attach a glue block to the work.

Parting
The act of severing the work from the lathe with a parting tool to cut a spindle turning at an appropriate point or to cut face work from the faceplate.

Parting tool
Tool for parting work from the lathe.

Pattern stick
A thin strip of wood on which a full-scale drawing of the piece to be turned is laid out. Notches at appropriate points allow the information on the pattern stick to be transferred to the work with a pencil.

Pin chuck
A metal dowel (pin) with a flat spot attached to a faceplate, which is inserted into a hole of like diameter drilled in the workpiece. A smaller pin is placed on the flat spot before the work is mounted on the dowel. The smaller pin cams sideways and locks the work on the dowel.

Planing cut
The cut made by a skew chisel when it's cutting properly (so called because the geometry of the cut is similar to that made by a hand plane).

Pressure turning
A chucking method in which the work is held on a glue block by the pressure of the tailstock spindle acting through a live center. It allows quick chucking and unchucking and leaves no marks on the work.

Rake angle
The angular distance from the top surface of the tool, just behind the cutting edge, to the surface of the work.

Reed
A bead that runs the length of a spindle turning rather than around it.

Rondel
A raised square ridge running around a spindle turning.

Roughing out
The act of bringing a square turning billet round.

Roughing-out gouge
A large U-shaped gouge for roughing out.

Scrape cut
The term has two meanings. One is when a normal turning tool is used incorrectly without the bevel rubbing. This entails presenting the tool at right angles to the work on the centerline rather than in a shear cut—a situation to be avoided. The second meaning is when a tool is intentionally sharpened to a burr and presented downhill. This is actually a shear cut because the burr is cutting at a highly positive angle.

Scraper
Any tool ground or burnished to a burr and presented downhill.

Screw chuck

A chuck consisting of a simple wood screw onto which the workpiece is threaded.

Scroll chuck

A metal chuck with three or four jaws that open or close in unison through the action of a scroll controlled by a key or levers.

Shear cut

A cut made when the bevel of a turning tool is presented tangentially to the surface of the work. This gives a positive-rake-angle cut that pares wood and leaves a good surface finish.

Skew chisel

A chisel with the edge skewed 15° to 20° from 90°.

Spindle

This term has two meanings. First, it can refer to any spindle-turned workpiece. Second, it refers to the shaft in either the headstock or tailstock. The headstock spindle is set in bearings and has a nose thread to accept faceplates. The tailstock spindle is often referred to as the "ram." Both spindles usually have Morse-taper sockets to accept accessories.

Spindle gouge

A gouge with a flute of constant radius and ground to a fingernail point. It is the basic tool of any spindle turner since it handles most spindle-turning situations.

Spindle turning

Any turning situation in which the grain of the workpiece runs parallel to the bed of the lathe.

Steady rest

A device that supports a spindle turning at some point near its center and dampens vibration, hence eliminating harmonic chatter.

Story stick

A thin strip of wood with notches cut at key points used in the layout of a spindle turning. It is a great aid in duplication.

Swing

The capacity of a lathe, which is twice the height of the center above the bed. The true capacity of any lathe, however, is the swing above the tool base.

Tailstock

A metal casting containing a spindle, or ram, that opposes the headstock. Its function is to hold pressure through a center on spindle work and to hold accessories such as drills while they act on work mounted on the headstock.

Tapered mandrel

A chuck that is a tapered (about 3°) rod. Hollow work can be held on a tapered mandrel for turning the outside of the piece.

Tearout

A surface imperfection produced when the grain is torn from the surface of the wood rather than pared away. This is most often a problem in the end grain of face work and requires heavy sanding to remove.

Tool base

A metal casting that attaches to the bed and holds the tool rest. It should lock solidly on the bed yet be able to be moved quickly and easily to any location or angle.

Tool rest

A T-shaped casting that mounts in the tool base and supports turning tools while they act on the workpiece.

Way

One of the two rails that form the lathe bed.

SOURCES OF SUPPLY

The following companies sell lathes, turning tools, various accessories, finishes and safety equipment, either through distributors or mail order. Many offer a catalog; call or write for cost and other information. Also listed are publishers of woodturning magazines, and companies and individuals who offer woodturning classes.

Airstream Dust Helmets
Highway 54 South
Elbow Lake, MN 56531
(800) 328-1792
(218) 685-4457

Air helmets and other safety equipment

American Association of Woodturners
667 Harriet Avenue
Shoreview, MN 55126
(612) 484-9094

American Woodturner magazine

American Woodcraft Tools
4425 Emery Industrial Parkway
Cleveland, OH 44128
(800) 433-5221
(216) 831-4404

Conover lathes

Arrowmont School of Arts and Crafts
Box 567
Gatlinburg, TN 37738
(615) 436-5860

Turning classes

Beech Street Tool Works
440 Beech Street
Los Angeles, CA 90065
(213) 223-0411

Stabilax and precision parting tools

Brookfield Craft Center
286 Whisconier Road
P.O. Box 122
Brookfield, CT 06804
(203) 775-4526

Turning classes

Conover Workshops
18125 Madison Road
P.O. Box 679
Parkman, OH 44080
(216) 548-3491

Turning classes

Constantine
2050 Eastchester Road
Bronx, NY 10461
(800) 223-8087

Lathes, turning tools and accessories; finishes, including shellac flakes

Craft Supplies USA
1287 E. 1120 S.
Provo, UT 84601
(800) 551-8876
(801) 373-0917

Lathes, turning tools, accessories; turning classes

Delta International Machinery Corp.
246 Alpha Drive
Pittsburgh, PA 15238
(800) 438-2486
(412) 963-2400

Lathes

Eagle America
124 Parker Court
P.O. Box 1099
Chardon, OH 44024
(800) 872-2511
(216) 286-9334

Lathes and accessories; special router bits for lathe work

David Ellsworth
Fox Creek
1378 Cobbler Road
Quakertown, PA 18951
(215) 536-5298

Turning classes

Garrett Wade Company
161 Avenue of the Americas
New York, NY 10013
(212) 807-1155

Lathes, turning tools and accessories

General Mfg. Co.
835 Cherrier Street
Drummondville, Quebec
Canada J2B 5A8
(819) 472-1161

Lathes

Glaser Engineering Co.
P.O. Box 95
El Segundo, CA 90245-0095
(310) 823-7128

Turning tools and screw chucks

Grizzly Imports
P.O. Box 2069
Bellingham, WA 98227
(800) 541-5537

Lathes, turning tools

Guild of Master Craftsmen
Castle Place
166 High Street
Lewes, East Sussex BN7 1XU
England
(800) 225-9262

Woodturning magazine

Highland Hardware
1045 N. Highland Avenue, NE
Atlanta, GA 30306
(800) 241-6748
(404) 872-4466

Lathes, turning tools and
accessories; turning classes

Lee Valley Tools
1080 Morrison Drive
Ottawa, Ontario
Canada K2H 8K7
(613) 596-0350

Lathes, turning tools and accessories

Oneway Manufacturing
241 Monteith Avenue
Stratford, Ontario
Canada N5A 2P6
(800) 565-7288
(519) 271-8441

Chucks, grinder rests, diamond
dressers

Rude Osolnik
P.O. Box 422
Berea, KY 40403
(606) 986-4440

Turning classes

Packard Woodworks
101 Miller Road
P.O. Box 718
Tryon, NC 28782
(704) 859-6762

Lathes, turning tools and accessories

Shopsmith
3931 Image Drive
Dayton, OH 45414-2591
(800) 543-7586
(513) 898-6070

Shopsmith combination lathe

Robert Sorby Ltd.
Athol Road/Woodseats Road
Sheffield S8 0PA
England
(0742) 554231

Turning tools

Trend-Lines
375 Beacham Street
Chelsea, MA 02150
(800) 767-9999

Lathes, turning tools, woodworking
supplies

Williams & Hussey Machine Co.
Souhegan Street
P.O. Box 1149
Wilton, NH 03086
(800) 258-1380
(603) 654-6828

Lathes

Woodcraft Supply Corp.
210 Wood County Industrial Park
P.O. Box 1686
Parkersburg, WV 26102-1686
(800) 225-1153

Lathes, turning tools and accessories

Woodworkers' Store
21801 Industrial Boulevard
Rogers, MN 55374-9514
(800) 279-4441
(612) 428-3200

Turning tools, specialty finishes

Woodworker's Supply
5604 Alameda Place, NE
Albuquerque, NM 87113-2100
(800) 645-9292

Lathes, turning tools, safety supplies,
finishes

Russ Zimmerman
RFD 3, Box 242
Putney, VT 05346
(802) 387-4337

Lathes and turning classes

INDEX

D

Dividers, for duplicating parts, 118
Drawer pull, turning, 170-175
Dressers, for grinder wheels, 72
Drill chuck. *See* Jacobs chuck.
Drilling:
    vs. boring, 136
    drill pad for, 137-138, 139
    in the headstock, 137-138
    with pod augers, 139
    in the tailstock, 136-137
    tool handles, 138
Drive centers, discussed, 34-36
Duplicating:
    calipers for, 116-117
    dividers for, 118
    lathe duplicators, 114
    masking tape for, 118
    open-end wrenches for, 117
    pattern stick for, 119-120, 121
    semaphores for, 117
    story stick for, 118, 120
    and tool shape, 120
Dust collection, systems for, 25
Dust protection, need for, 31

E

Electrical safety, discussed, 30
Electrical service, discussed, 25-26
Eye protection, need for, 31

F

Faceplates:
    custom-made, 40
    and "flyers," 40
    jam chucks for, 51
    materials for, 39
    modifying, 40, 41
    securing work to, 40-42, 178
    seized, removing, 152-154
    sizes of, 39-40
    tapered mandrels for, 55

Faceplate turning:
    glue blocks for, 59
    with green wood, 101
    paper joints for, 128, 129
    pressure-chucking for, 60-61
    and sanding, 124
    speeds for, 30
    vs. spindle turning, 32, 34
    tools for, 90-94
    See also Faceplates.
Finial, turning, 160-169
Finishing:
    with French polish, 126-127, 169,
        173, 185
    process of, 125-127
Flutes:
    cutting, 131, 133
    jig for, 132
    laying out, 133
    See also Index head. Reeds.
Form tools:
    beads with, 121, 167
    captive rings with, 122
    making, 120
French polish, applying, 126-127,
    169, 173, 185

G

Gap, of lathe bed, described, 12
"Ghost," reading, 100, 120
Glue blocks:
    chucking with, 59, 134-135
    See also Pressure turning.
        Screw chucks, shopmade.
Gouges. *See* Bowl gouge. Roughing-
    out gouge. Spindle gouge.
Grind angle, of tool, 64
Grinders:
    guards for, 71
    lighting at, 71
    rests on, 68-70
    safety shields on, 70-71
    sizes of, 68
    wheels for, 71-72
        dressing, 72
    See also Sharpening.

Grinding:
    process of, 73
    See also Grinders. Sharpening.

H

Headstock:
    aligning with tailstock, 19-20
    bearings in, 13-14, 143
    centers for, 34-36
    disassembling, 143-144
    faceplates for, 39-42
    index head for, 15-16
    Morse tapers in, 10
    for outboard turning, 14-15
    raising, 156
    spindles of, 10-12
    See also Tailstock.
Honing:
    process of, 74
    whetstones for, 73-74
    See also Buffing. Grinding.

I

Index head, features of, 15-16
Ivory nut. *See* Tagua.

J

Jacobs chuck, discussed, 49
Jam chucks:
    making, 50-53
    using, 54
Jigs, for cutting flutes and reeds,
    132

L

Lathes:
    benchtop, 7
    bow, 8-9
    cast-iron, advantages of, 4
    construction of, 4-6
    design of, 2
    drilling in, 136-139
    duplicators for, 114
    electrical requirements for, 25
    extruded aluminum, 6

Editor: PETER CHAPMAN

Designer/Layout Artist: JODIE DELOHERY

Illustrator: ORIGINAL DRAWINGS BY ERNIE CONOVER,
REDRAWN BY MARIA MELESCHNIG, EXCEPT WHERE NOTED

Photographer, except where noted: ERNIE CONOVER

Copy/Production Editor: PAM PURRONE

Art Assistant: ILIANA KOEHLER

Typeface: GARAMOND

Paper: WARREN PATINA MATTE, 70 lb., NEUTRAL pH

Printer: ARCATA GRAPHICS/HAWKINS, NEW CANTON, TENNESSEE